WHAT THE WORLD NEEDS NOW

ANTHONY GUZMAN

What The World Needs Now
By **Anthony Guzman**
@anthonyguzmanpoetry

Copyright © 2023 Anthony Guzman

Edited by **Eva Xan**

Designed by **Keyla Brando**

Cover art by **Anthony Guzman**

— Introduction —

In *What the World Needs Now*, I learn to embrace the spirits of nature as my own: as teachers, scholars, guides, masters of their medicine, counselors to both wounded and happy souls, and bridge-builders between soul and soul.

This book has taught me that Earth is a playground, and if we don't play in it, we'll all be unhappy, depressed, bored, and continue to irrigate our problems. I have witnessed that when humankind walks through life without a purpose, we are more destructible in our state of mind and in the actions we take, painting over the land. Learning about myself and my relationship with God makes me a purposeful, richer human being.

In this book, I bring the spirit of nature into my heart and into my home. I've found solitude in her, so I've written her a letter of forgiveness, a poetic apology for the harm that's been inflicted upon her by some souls on the earth. I've found ways to redesign myself in the same way the seasons give trees new names, leaves, and birthdays. I've been inspired by how the stars stare at me. I also wrote poems to the moon in order to be risen by steps made of poems, to chill in a hammock, exchanging my full presence and attention and ultimately making time disappear.

The primary purpose of *What the World Needs Now* is to open our hearts by sealing our eyes so we can remember the important aspects of worshipping devotionally and what our heart invites inward and processes. I believe we can make God dance and the earth walk once again naked; we can make them trust humankind.

I was drawn to Shamanism by the mystery of my curiosity and my personal departure from religion due to its heavy dominance over controlling human ways of worship and my personal belief that there is no need for an in-between when communicating with the source of all being. I have found that Shamanism has the spiritual description that has brought out the best in me. With my ancestral poetic talents granted by God, I place them in your hands to travel to your hearts. Have you ever felt so empty that the only thing that fills you is Essence? The answers to your questions are written in the details of trees...

I learn to empty my mind by interchanging the space in the sky with the clouds in my mind. Can you put your trust in a land that was designed to not only feed your stomach but also your soul?

I have been on the hunt to figure out this word: oneness. Oneness is a reality that binds all life together in an endless web crocheted by love and torn by no one. Nature has taught me how to heal.

And to advance with a new set of beliefs and realities, the truth is that we are all victims, inflicting wounds concisely and unconsciously on each other. In equal measure, we are builders of gardens that once lacked love who all carry the medicine we need within.

This poetry collection reminds me that we give meaning to our lives from the curiosity of our imagination, not from the basket of our unsettled minds or indecisive desires. Mother Earth is a masterpiece that humanity must preserve in the museum stored in our hearts. We must hand this down to the next generation by how we educate them to treat the earth and themselves as well.

Sometimes, I believe that societal programming has stolen the one-on-one experience we should be having with the moon and the stars, with the sun and our eyes. Have you ever had an animal knock on your door and ask you if you needed advice? In Shamanism, this doesn't mean you see things or make up lies. This is a sign of the spirit calling, so get ready, enjoy, and trust the ride. I want to bring a type of food, a kind of perspective, and a feeling of joy to the reader, so I dedicate my time and craft to lovers of art, nature, and ancient spiritual seekers.

I also believe there is a reason for our continual questioning. Some curiosities are best left alone to not spoil our drive. So, I'd rather be the unknown's passenger and a lover of God's love, a thankful witness of everyone's evolving into the butterfly that fits in today. And the snakes seem to be punish and misjudge for speaking universal truth. But I'd rather be the omen of life: the crow that admires life from a spacious perspective; the center of my simplicity and kindness, walking like a giraffe; a student of Buddha becoming a layback turtle; a Taoist sloth accepting nature's pace; and a Sufi snail circling our God's heart.

See, nature's got a ton to share with us! But if we are stabbing the teacher (who is ready to grade us on the ways we relate to her), we will never pass her class. So I say, join your love, join your passion, join your action, join your forgiveness, and don't forget why God designed us on this beautiful earth, our true home. Chamanismo is another language for hearing God's voice and the needs of your heart and earth.

We are here to place another rock on top of the pile of life. God doesn't belong to a set of beliefs or a specific religion or individual, but to everyone. I'm a mosaic surrounded by powerful animals; I'm the center of a clock, and the numbers around me are animals. Our lives are borrowed books from a library, and we are in control of the maintenance and condition of every seam binding our existence. Life is a gift no one can steal from you.

When Mother earth calls, I answer, leaving the tribe that I no longer belong to. I've been in love with animals since my trip to a farm. I was once again drafted by spiritual guides to enter the woods of my home, between the brick walls and the curtain I didn't hang. I seek my identity by riding a rocket ship into my history. I discovered my ancestors in numerous streams lost in the ocean of mountains. God made me an exotic being.

Have you ever felt misunderstood by relatives and condemned by society as a result of your questions? What does freedom mean to you? I found my peace in nature. My power animals and my ancestors reminded me that I do not walk alone, and the great shaman told me that I'm a disciple of love.

An example of tranquility that everybody sees in me. On this journey through books and visions, I seek the path that enlightenment shares with me with a cup of tea. Sometimes I'm down, and sometimes I'm up. But isn't that what being human means?

In *What the World Needs Now*, I share a poetic version of me: my relationship with nature, my communication with my ancestors, my devotion to The One, the dance I share with my animals' powers... Every time, I meditated with a question of some sort, stimulating my brain with possible wisdom that I consume like my medicine.

In this book is the practice I had to develop with intention that brought me clarity, along with some deeper questions about my purpose and spiritual preference as well as my relationship with the animals that I could relate to in various ways. When the great shaman speaks, I get out of bed! My shoes get tied. I'm motivated to press on and run over fresh grass. I am reminded that life is more than just clocking in and clocking out. Outside my room, there is a fantastical world, another dimension where I am ready to serve my spiritual physician and fulfill my mental request to transform. With an empty stomach and a curious mind, I discover freedom on my path. With a love for nature since kindergarten, I'm called to retreat into it to find the answers to the questions that gave birth to new transformations.

My first introduction to Shamanism was in this book I came across when I was in college called "Ecoshamanism" by James Endredy. I was eager and willing to discover and prove to myself that there was more to a standing tree and there were mysterious connections in the way I breathed into the sky and the earth with all the elements around me. I needed there to be a name for this way of life, for this philosophy. But I didn't know what it was called yet...

What the World Needs Now is a poetic story that narrates my shamanic interests and background influences and helps ground my past with the present. A walk in the woods simply brings back a fundamental and ancient way of life. There is magic; there's something incredible; something is continually unfolding. This changes when you trust the divine, the universe, god, and spirit guides on the spiritual path I have chosen to live by.

Some people ask why we kill ourselves by working so much. Is it truly for a cause? Well, I say the experiences and steps we take along the way comprise the masterpiece that we are today. I believe that no day is wasted, and that every bad experience can be recycle into a good one.

With this poetry collection, I construct the masterpiece that am today. There is no such thing as a wasted day or a bad experience that we cannot turn into a good one. God puts us all in different battles in order to blend the you that awaits your enlightenment.

— ALONE TIME WITH THE WATER —

Yemaya Landscape

At sea,
we are preserved pearls
that comfort dolphins;
deep holes in the sea
that store wounds.
We seek to be fish,
hard heads becoming fluid
as waves hammer into coconut shells.

Above the sea,
I see how we should live:
next to God, watching palms
dance with the beach.

Untamed

The cleansing of every pearl
starts when we become the water mill.

No one can claim your waters.
They may try
but fail like an anxious ship
tied to a newly installed anchor.

God stirs in you
minerals that cleanse home
without needing man-made detergent
that spoils wooden floors.

Visions in my head swim like telescope gold fish.
Seated on a water cushion,
your sand massages my body.
You are the vibration that moves the whole ocean.

Trust the Bumps

Yemaya, clean my hands of all mischief.
My eyes may store rotten pearls,
and they can't live in beautiful shells.

Yemaya, cleanse my hands with the first wave
that touches the earth.
I form and actions emerge
from the tip of my unknowing desires.

Yemaya, I am behind your tail,
catching blessings
and pursuing you across the seas.
I'm learning how we are connected,
even by the currents of the sea.

Yemaya, touch me with the first wave.
You move the soil.
Faith has the ability to construct human ships
that can skip over paradoxical streams.

I have learned to trust.
All the waves God launches at me
with new sense
feel every bump like a newborn
under the cushion of his first stroller.
It feels like he's still in the womb
of his mother.

Student of the Sea

Yemaya, I come to you.

How I got into the hands of my wife,
how children arrive...
Birth gives form to another part of the sea.

How food falls into acidic bellies,
how I get to my job,
how I get to my house...
Life is a lean and a rock.

I come to you because you once crashed into me.

How grandma's feet touch the ground.
The sea water has an effect on me.
How does water reach the sands
and how do new shells appear on beaches?

New things in life
give me more reasons to live,
but none of them belong to me.
Neither bought nor given,
but I still must religiously take care of them.
Life keeps leaning and rocking,
and I'm unable to control the rhythm that invites me.

Oceanic Prayer

Yemaya, my body is your home—.
my poems, shells in your sand.
Erase the actions in me that cause me to drift
like an imperfect ship.
Let my entrance be the breeze on every beach.
Quicksand desires the love of my heart.
Pierce me with swordfishes
so I can be reborn as a new fish.

Guardian of pregnant mermaids,
you guard God's children as if they were pearls.
Cleanse the fragments of my soul
and polish my fear
so I can face them
like a crab resisting aggressive winds.

Hydrated by Faith

I'll wait for you
like sand waiting for waves to move her.
I'll wait for you like crabs
that await you to return them to the sea.
I'll wait for you on the shore of my sadness
so you can take me
to the island of my new happiness.

I offer you melons and candles
and white roses of love.
I wait for the most tender waves
to return my thankfulness as a Child of God.
A pearl in this massive ocean,
I have learned to trust you with the silence of my heart
and the thirsty scales of my yearning body.

Constantly Changing

The seagulls wet their feet in your water.
As I watch my face on your breast,
engines on every boat love massaging your back.
Diving into you, they arrive at their destination.

Take away my letters about worthless things
because I trust you.
Fishes find their home under your water
and forget that a world exists outside of your stream.

We are all exchanging oxygen,
but are we sharing love in the same way?
People find their peace of mind watching your waves
and listen to music while you feature new songs with rocks.
Meditation is my headphone, and I get lost in my own song.
The earth sits next to you in class,
and God teaches you about the mystery of your elements.
I try to take notes in detail, but ink can't encapsulate it.
Life is meant to be lived, not explained.

The sun, the clouds, the stars, and the moon
consider you to be their mirror.
They look down and reflect.
on how much they have grown
since yesterday, since last year,
since the beginning of time.

Yemaya, you are the mirror
I can always look in
to embrace where I started,
acknowledging who I am tonight,
who I was today,
and who may I be tomorrow.
I am changing daily
like the clouds under the sun.

Coconut and Candles

Yemaya, lift me up with your waves.
Baptize me in the rivers I enter.

Assist me in bringing the light
to say goodbye to my night.

Erase my wounds with pearls that shine like stars.
Let's stop anxiety from laying eggs in the soul.

I want to know how the world works.
Teach me to crash into God
like the rivers and oceans crash into you.

Seagulls sing a song that makes the sun
open the curtain on every ocean floor.

Yemaya, I am the blue candle
placed in this coconut
and protected by the waters.

God cries every day
so waves can rise
and purify my heart.

Calling Waves

I sit on a yoga mat over a rock
by this lucid river,
waiting for the transparency of my voice.
I am aware that I am not alone;
I know I'm not the only soul
who has been here before,
who is here *now*.

When I look around
I reflect on my environment,
taking note of the shadows and visions of other souls.
Children of Yemaya are all around me.
Yemaya, your waves call us to the bay of your soul.
The spirit god painted me
and claims to wave with you.

I offer you watermelon with seven shiny pennies,
each one representing a different aspect of yourself.
The ocean's chakras connect me to you.
Align me to every water stream
that take my eyes on canoe trips.
I need to be the shell
and soak in your lighthouse once again.
As your waves dance to the beat of my maraca,
I once again awaken you.

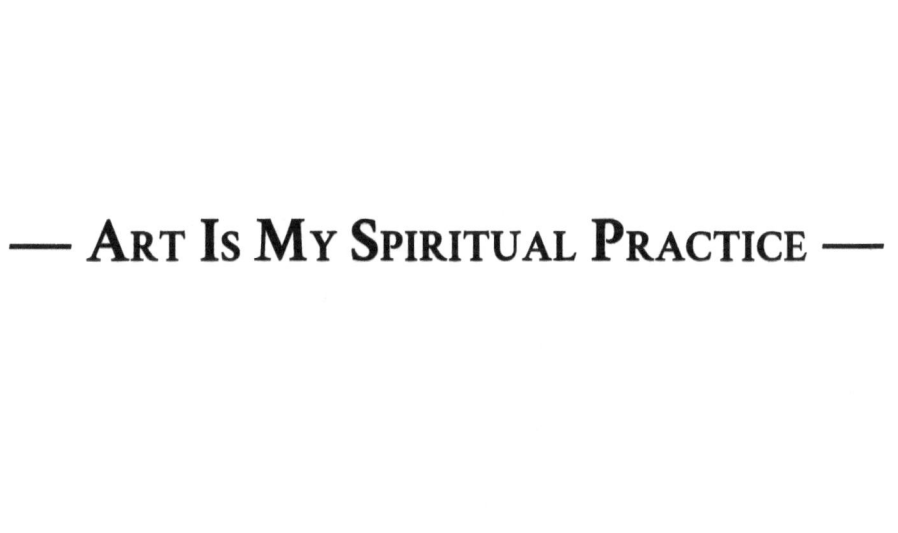

— ART IS MY SPIRITUAL PRACTICE —

The Purpose of Art

It is a great pursuit to design casually.
Yet it is even more important to design with respect.
Respectfully designing expands creativity.
Designing with disrespect shortens your creativity's lifespan.
A respectable artist understands that art has an impact on /
everyone.
the same way it has an effect on themselves.
If the effect is bad, a respectful artist would correct the /
message of his craft,
understanding that the energy behind a formation
is more important than getting rich off of someone's /
deformity.
Art should move the world positively.

Nature advises that you not to rush the drying process /
of your artwork.
Can't you see that the flowers aren't shaking off?
The raindrops, they waited so long to feel.

Art is how I take the time to understand God's formula /
of creation.
I stick to being a student of art without trying to remove
the master from the realm of inspiration.
Art makes me become an admirer, storing away /
the judge in me.
Art teaches me how to consciously create myself
for the betterment of myself and my surroundings.
Art finds all the ways to kill the spirit of boredom.

When I take the time to understand the details of art,
I get lost in the present moment of understanding
and different parts of the emotional dimensions.

Art challenges me to capture what many artists have /
captured before me.
Art teaches me how to express myself authentically /
and honestly.
Art is what dresses up our existence with emotions
that come out of beauty and sacrifice.
Beauty is inspired by the seen and unseen.
Beauty symbolizes the illusion of perfection
and the spiritual reality of impermanence and abstraction.

Art is the cry of a rainbow hidden behind magnificent valleys.
Art is a brightly colored grenade launched from a /
humid forest.
Art is a visual demonstration of what if,
A Visual Revolution!
A visual suggestion that may be difficult to grasp in numbers.

Art is the mastery of reconstructing
and deconstructing concepts and themes
that existed from the beginning of man's spiritual intelligence.
Art lets us all relate to different parts of God's /
abstract creation.

Surprise Yourself More Often

Express yourself to become yourself.

Express yourself to be a part of the sound of oneness.

Express yourself, accept your beauty, accept your all,
and put away the ugly that doesn't work.

Express yourself to find yourself.
When life throws you clouds that cover your entire force,
mold out of that doom, turning everything around you /
into a cocoon,
and become the boom that makes you bloom.

Express yourself to heal someone who once was you.

Express yourself so your voice can be heard by someone /
who admires art.

Express yourself to become the instrument that was meant /
to be listened to.

Express yourself as a representative of the Great Spirit.

Express yourself to bloom on your walk,
like glowing fish in the deepest parts of the earth.

Express yourself in your own form
with the medium that challenges you,
with the microphone you were once afraid to use.

Express yourself with your gift to unwrap magical things,
becoming God's puppet and emerald ball,
trusting the movement of the earth.

Express yourself respecting yourself in others and /
others in you.

Express yourself to have revelations and reflections.

Express yourself as if you were a newborn baby.
Expand your fingers like aliens.
Expand your feet like duck's quack and make beautiful noise:
the sound of a temple chanting love,
a whale back-flipping in your backyards,
a whisper of bees constructing shelter for honey.

Express yourself as if you were in love with everything /
and everyone,
which makes expressing yourself more spiritual.

Express yourself because you have access to universal truth

Express yourself in order to depress your adversary
by what you confess because life isn't a silent courtroom,
but rather God's successful musical creation.

Express yourself with the power to undress
anything that weighs down
that should be floating above water.

Express yourself because you know
you're still a work in progress
and not a complete piece.

My Dress Form

Dress to attract yourself,
to give your spirit a chance
to repossess the peace lily that was stolen
from the garden of kindness.

Don't cage your creativity out of fear.
Let your art set you free!
Bench press visions that rest in pigment.
God knows that we should
share our individuality.

Dress to attract yourself,
and your art will stand without oppressing others.
True to the prep that molds a new scream,
from actions that whisper
from your heart to your mind.

Be you and only you
so you won't have to be a clone,
a popular imitation,
a sister who was abducted by
a plastic surgeon waiting room,
choking God's natural recipe
away from your natural creation.

Be yourself and only yourself
to empower your presence.
on the earth of our mother.
Have fun with every other creation
while keeping your own style
out of the exchange of clones
without a voice.

Every Artistic Session

Art is the language of the artist.
Art is the thing that knocks the bell off of my brain
and fills the basement of my body.
Art is the noise interrupting silence.
Art is the melody that raises the spiritless.
Art is the mirror that draws me back.
Art reminds me of who I am.

Art is a still photo moving in scenes as I grow.
Art paints on me smiles with golden pastel permanent marker,
washing away sadness with watercolor.
Art is a placenta protecting the artist.
Art does not lie to you.
Art is a new devotion born of old feelings,
where my body serves as the canvas
and my time is transformed into a temple.

Art is the truth that doesn't even fit in courtrooms.
Art is how God preaches to me.
The earth teaches me
how to lose myself in order to find broken balance
to repair and varnish.
Art unmutes the soul.
Art is the bait that makes me rise
from my lows to the surface of my high.

Art is my spiritual practice.
Art is the way God watches me age.
Art is the way in which
I watch my art mature in others.

Art is where my tears fall,
where you can find the whole me.
Art can be rehabilitate me in an hour.
It's a minute of therapy
and everything in one second of inspiration.
Art is my spiritual practice.
It's the part of me you shouldn't be afraid to see.
because it is the most humane part of me.

Musical Therapy

I know a drum
that wants to be heard; pick her up.
If you, the artist decide
to open up their skin too,

I know a maraca
that's got a grip,
that wants to rhyme and shake down walls.

I know a harmonica
that wishes someone would blow on her form
so everyone can hear her soul.

I know a viola that heals, and when she cries
from the stroke, you pass her a napkin,
healing the nervous system of your body.

I know an oud guitar
that generates the sounds.
of hidden dreams.

I know an erhu violin
that calms the tears
of a baby dropped off at daycare.

I know a saxophone
that can make anyone
believe in love again.

I know a singing bowl
that sings like a baby in the womb
of a peaceful mother connecting daily with the unseen.

I know an acoustic guitar
that can write a whole
album in one song.

I know a sitar
that can reset an anxious body
and turn it into clouds that trust the sky again.

I know a tempura guitar
that can silence
all gossip.

I know a didgeridoo
that can scare away demons,
opening runway shows for angels into my heart.

I know a violin that can
make my poems cry
and inspire new ways in which I paint my day.

I know flutes
that can make me fly
from the Andes to Asia
while I'm walking in NYC.

I know a piano
that mummified rush hour
and became my poetry teacher;
I get lost in the casket of her voice.

Instruments were made for me
to take trips on them
as I journey into the unknown.

I'm a Part of Your Dreams

Now is the time to dream up
the role you want to play.

Loosen up with your friends or by yourself
because all we have are these colors
that reflect the origin of every pigment,
making our dreams
native to the realm of love.

Allow each day to be a witnessing studio.
Make the best out of everything.
Don't make small things big—
neither big thing bigger than the other.

Find new songs to jam to
so my style of poetry
finds new homes.

Every day, meditate to weave
once more a circle of love,
where we can coexist
in the biggest book made out of one page.

Tie my shoes to play in this moment
on my playground.
Walking on virgin grass,
the soles of my feet are being massaged
by the nerves on leaves.

They influence each other
indirectly and directly.
Can you imagine the masterpiece?
Everyone is going to admire it
while we sit next to each other.

Married to My Discipline

Life is a constant movement.
Sometimes, I play death
to escape for a minute or a second,
eliminating disharmony in me
to rediscover my inner peace.
My breathing has become
the new way that I move;
It tames my body.

When nerves try to harness me,
I nurture the soul
by listening to instruments
and relearning how to breastfeed
in contact with God
and the universe I create in me
with my eyes closed.

I fly to places only I know.
Because I have the ability
to change all of the mattresses at home,
but if I'm not comfortable
or in love with the cushion
of my own body, mind, and soul,
I'll never sleep in peace
on any branded source.

I'm the masterpiece.
I have to varnish
and self-feed the soul,
even if the spoons carry crumbs.

I've been grounded in God's love.
I'm the sunflower that worships the sun,
following the orange
across the globe.
No one can cut my roots,
only the radiating spiral of love.

No medical machine understands the body's pain.
Only God can determine the weight of my process.
Even when I'm not alone, I walk fearfully at times,
shifting my focus to certainty.

I try to look at life
with the same eyes that a newborn
examines his mother's nipples with.
Life is a constant movement;
I must yield to the Tao
and listen to the orchestra of God,
loving the instruments that enlighten
the ears of my eyes
as I fall in love with my
never-ending discipline.

God's Alarm Clock

Have you stopped giving thanks
to Mother Nature and the Ancestors
who have given thanks
once upon a time
for remembering them?

You should
increase your artistic expression
and speak your happiness.
Talk your poetry;
Let your spirit be heard.
Listen to your voice.
If it has kind things to say
to the flesh,
you belong to today.

Don't hide in
the silence of ignorance.
Excessive ambition
speeds up your death certificate,
making you miss the precious moments
you can't buy with a routing number.
The morning shows me the beginning of life
all over again in different sounds that we can't buy.

Speak of your heart's joy;
Don't silence the truth.
Awaken your personality
all over again in a whole different way.

You are still alive
in a body fragmented by suffering
but healed by love within positive faith.

Have you forgotten
why God has woken you up
this morning once again?
Don't be anxious.

Take God's classes once more
and paint the best canvas.
out of your new day.

Dreamer

Don't try leading the waves
that create their own streams.

Instead, let the waves of the ocean lead you.
Don't interrupt the steps of your dreams
by standing in front of them with tough words.

Dreamer, lead your dreams!
Don't let other dreamers lead them for you.
Only you know the chant of your tears.

Dreamer, merge with the force
behind the current and follow the waves.
Your destiny desires to crash with you.

Don't run on fuel that contaminates;
Use your own source and energy.

Reflect clearly
with the hunger of a baby
and the new connection
made from milk-bonding,
reflecting memories created in the womb.
Dreamer, I have learned not to rush.
Art has taken its time
soaking me in different worlds of patience.

Dreamers, wet your brush with
tears and faith.
You'll see how God mops
your path to success.

Dreamer, listen to the echo
of your true desire.
Let God become the bait
as you ride your rails into
a mystery with no clear path.

Dreamers let things fall into place.
Return to the blueprint for Every Rising Step.
Just be the first step in every moment you escalate.

Dreamer's construction without friction is a waste.
There must be yin and yang
to every taste,
to each and every sweat.

Dreamer, it's your dream to discover
what's inside you first
before you chase external things.

DESIGN

Design to make the world a better place.
Design to influence other dreamers.
Design to move and inspire neighboring tribes.
Design to add to the harmony of the world.
Design to move with the spirit of the universe.
Design to contribute to the awakening.
Design to spark love in people.
Create in order to enlighten people.
Design to water the roots of the people.
Design to unite the people.

Let the environment feed our purpose.
Let the journey be the spoon that feeds our presence
and use the same spoon to feed the environment
for the teachings it has shared with us,
helping us overcome personal and universal challenges.

Design to remind yesterday that today is possible.
Design to tighten the screw
that we didn't have enough force to seal alone.

Be Weird

I was sent here
to ornament your boredom.

I was thrown here.
to leap like a rainbow.

I was placed here
to design myself a little differently from you.

I was born here.
To promote my sprouting out of the earth as sage

I am an advancement of the things
you won't do from the nature of your heart.

I was dispatched here at the last point
where my ancestors left behind their bravery.

I wasn't cast here to please you;
I was cast here to please Spirit.

I was sent here for the same reason you were sent here:
to spend life discovering the purpose

Why did Mom risk her life giving birth to me
and why did Dad decide not to pull out
as He cast a life-giving spell in a virgin's pot?

I was designed so I could keep decorating myself
with the things nature gives birth to and adorns herself in.

I was thrust from the womb into this world
to find my soul in every other form that exists here with me.

I was sent here to be different,
a stimulator of perspectives.

I was sent here so you could question normality
and then set yourself self free.

A Thankful Son

When people around me
turn into falcons,
I recharge inside a crow's nest.

Inspired by rainbow serpents,
I drag all my art supplies
through the floor to see if I give roses
a vision that seizes your eyes
so you fall in love and give art its true value.

I chant and meditate
while I'm inside a squirrel's tree,
snacking on acorns
and telling the world in front of my eyes
where I would climb next,

The morning is a puddle of snail slime;
It doesn't let me move
if I don't start my morning with a grateful
and graceful meditation,
kissing my bedsheet goodbye.

Everyone moves on top
of the earth according to
the weight of their own slime.

While I meditate, I extend my neck
as if a giraffe has become my masseuse,
the height of my capabilities is God,
and the foundation on my peace is the earth.

I try to introduce myself to the morning
as light as possible,
listening to the birds
sing for me and sing to the ones
that appreciate Mother Nature's
playlist for all.

— **DREAMING MY REALITY** —

You Look like a Whole Different Nigga

My body and thoughts
had being dying to ask the universe
some spiritual questions.

I escaped four years of learning
from the streets
and now I needed to wander in
a new space
that was getting filled
by potential answers.

The spiritual questions:
1. Why am I wasting time?
2. Where is the oneness of all life that exists?
3. What does it mean to be one with all
one with god?
4. What is my personal definition of love?
Every definition of love was so fucked up...

Yesterday's Breeze

Past events,
lovers, friends;
experiences, demons,
bad deeds and challenging jobs.

Don't try to present yourself
today as if you were my new event.
I'm the percent of nature
that flows according to growth.

I have fought dragons and bats
and left them cemented in the night

to find peace in the morning
and repent for my past,
drinking tea with the sun
that cracks my window open.

I won't let you interrupt
my presence's state, my present scent.
Now life compliments me.

My heart now depends
on a mind no one can torment
because I spend my faith in divine love
and today I represent
who I couldn't be yesterday.

I invent my intent
to vent, fermenting my soul
with the life that witnesses
the breeze of my growth.

Who I Was Yesterday, Who I Am Today

Yesterday, a lot of people died.
Today, the same amount
of people are born all over the world with a new birthday.

Yesterday, I understood the world for one second.
Today, I wake up and understand the world
as an essay.

Yesterday, I loved myself outwardly.
Today, I love myself for who I am inwardly.

Yesterday, the clouds were against me.
Today, those clouds cover me like palm leaves.

Yesterday, I didn't believe in beauty.
Today, beauty opens my road,
and I start seeing beyond gray.

Yesterday, I walked alone.
Today, I walk with animals that guard me
in this living dream as a dreamcatcher hung on clouds.

Yesterday, I didn't acknowledge my ancestors.
Today, I accept that my ancestors are always around me
so I must not disobey.

Yesterday, I swam on the surface of life.
Today, I play on the ocean floor of life.

Yesterday, I was dying while I was living.

Today, I'm living to die like that part of me
that ran away but somehow stayed.

Yesterday, I knew less.
Today, I know a tiny bit more,
but I still can't grasp the x-ray
of this whole cosmic beauty I exist in.

Yesterday, I had a lot of friends.
Today, I just walk with a few allies.
In between all of my yesterdays
and all my todays, all I can make of it
is a Milky Way.

The Rising Warrior

Warrior, grow up.
Come out of the mountains and inner caves,
and make your body vibrate.

Your heart tells you best.
The spiritual armory is
the Great Spirit blacksmith in the pattern of your being.

Can your intention
set your purpose free,
aligning you to the mission carved on your cup?

Rise up and clean up
what your heart says is wrong,
what your heart says is right.

Rise up!
Give yourself a chance
to be a part of this great spiritual battle.

Rise up, rise up
with your intentions clearly lit by the sunlight
and sketch them out by moonlight.

Rise up, rise up, warrior,
to continue the fight
you have decided to warm-up.

Rise up, rise up,
so the next pup
can continue the fight
with their head up.

Undressing My Ego

Everything looks better naked.
Strip away from egos!
Detach yourself from dressed up egos
that were once influenced
by other egos
that were also playing
dress up.

Everything looks better naked.
There's no need to waste time
trying to figure out:
people's collection of faces
hiding behind their true identity.

Everything looks better naked.
I feel more joy and care less for judgment
as I try my best to walk on this earth as I came:
naked, and more naked away from lies,
closer to meditating.

Everything looks better naked.
The earth is a bathtub
that we forget to properly bathe our souls in.
Dive into the spirit of the earth,
and you would see
that we all bathe in her nakedness.
Be one with the soap
that cleanses our heart
and reconditions our minds.

Under No Disguise

Live under your true mask.
If you have a chance to escape,
choose the one you live in to survive.

Live from your wild side.
instead of someone else's
silent lifestyle.

Live by the codes of your heart
and not the fishing road of boredom.

Follow the lotus of peace,
not an antisocial cactus.

Live by the rules of the divine
and the ways of nature
to inspire the Tao to become a waterfall.

Live under the colors of your mask,
not by someone else's fading pigments.

Live up to your most profound potential.
Even if the entire mountain hikes,
test your devotion and practice.

Live enveloped in divinity,
not in man-made chaos.

Live in love with the dream you are slowly molding,
not the one that collapses rapidly; stick to something.

Dance under the power of your mask
and be possessed by the rules of true love
beyond human description.

Become the seam behind honesty
and just be true to yourself—
to bring light to a society,
layers of soulless bodies.

Even though the movies are not playing
how you expected them to,
don't speed up the scenes in them;
you'll catch the lessons.

Live in accordance with the seasons of nature,
not the promotion of stocks and lottery prizes.

Live by the song of your faith,
not by the destructor of humanity.

Live to make God smile,
not allowing evil to flourish.

In all honesty, live to cry
for your needs crushing unneeded things.

Live to make your household a temple
and life a dome that witnesses your love.

Live in accordance with the orchestra of creation,
not a field of nuclear domination.

Live without ignoring your sentimental part.
Make life softer and more fluid to break
into each other's lives like crumbs
of bread without an identity.

Live by the substance of spirituality,
not by a recitation of experience without essence.

Live according to your accomplishments,
not by the memories hunting you down.

Live because today is ready to take you on a walk
and always remind you that you are prepared,
even if you don't believe it.

Live outside the system of anxiety—
on the yoga mat that connects you to the divine lungs.

Live your life,
blowing into one another.
Love
like a flutist
who blows all of himself into a pipe.
He sacrificed to tranquilize our existence;
I dream my reality.

The Seeds of Experience

As you walk,
as you live,
as you learn,
as you fall,
as you grow,
you are planting seeds—

from the seeds you have lived
to the seeds you live today
and the seeds you'll leave behind.

Some seeds will die,
some seeds will get to see the light,
some seeds will teach you new things,
some seeds will teach you old things,
some seeds will teach you patience,
some seeds will just be surprises,
some seeds you won't get to see again
on the journey of life...

When you breathe, you plant;
when you laugh, you plant;
when you cry, you plant;
when you suffer, you plant;
when you dream, you plant;
when you take your steps, you plant;
when you find your freedom, you plant...

Your seeds will leave behind markings—
markings that unfold from the gift of life,
the gift of existence
the gift of being,
the gift of experiencing,
the gift of living and loving...

So take your bag of seeds
and plant consciously
without expectations.

The Inner Child

There's a kid within us
who always wants to play.
Don't ignore
the child within you,
and I won't ignore that child in me;
it just wants to play.

Let's set ourselves free
from our old flesh
and never age.
Play a game
that would make us younger
in this old world
of old things
perceived in new ways.

Let's bring our toys
and run to the woods.
Let's become planes and cars,
flying and racing,
making our bodies feel fresh
as we step on this minty earth.

Don't let aging
erase your innocence.
Don't let your innocence
run loose.
Be like the kid
they call a delinquent—
the curious, the weird, the questionable

of the whole group.
Because if you are like that kid,
you are living life to the fullest.

Dig into the cookie jar of life
because there's a kid within us
who always wants to play.
Stop sitting down
during careers and professions.
Get up, you vintage toy!
Fall down again, duckling,
like when you were a little kid.

Laugh and never lose
the kid within you
who always wants to play...

Sweetness Kills Bitterness

We all need to exchange some words
and hug the ones we never spoke to before.
Kiss me with the stories of wisdom and history.
Leave lines of love marked on my forehead
so I can remember how far I've come from.
Love dies daily to feed our hunger.

We live in a world of dreamers,
but not every dreamer gets to see their dream.
Hug, kiss, talk to me.
Wake my dreams up,
even if I don't get to see them!

We must all sit down, talk, hug, and kiss
the nighttime goodbye.
We must let the moon know we are satisfied
because there are
thousands of temples and homes missing affectionate stars.

Let's not lock our capabilities of freeing ourselves
from the shyness of our senses.
Let's quilt together humanity
and swing each other in the cover of our skins.
Let's surprise today with the manifestation
of what could have been yesterday.

Let's release tension from our spines and necks
and destroy the systems oppressing our capabilities.
Let's hug, kiss, and talk
be each other's medicine—

medicine filling me,
medicine curing you...
God prescribes the recipe.

Maybe if I speak to you talk more often;
maybe if I hug you as often,
that'll help us
invite sweetness
where solitude and privacy
has laid down
too much bitterness and inhumanity.

Stronger Than I Think

Bad acts
and bad thoughts
leave my mind

like the abused child runs out
from his father's house,
becoming a man
in the streets;

like a girl in love
running away with her first boyfriend
that everyone rejects.

Bad acts
and bad thoughts
leave my mind.

Don't dirty or damage
the new steps that the holiness
of my new perception creates.

My consciousness
has finally risen higher than yesterday,
and I will not return to the behavior of "fuck it."

I know now that
after the storm
new fruits are born
who learn to endure
where they couldn't hold on to before.

Snake Dance

I'm like the snake
radiating vibration.

If my vibe is good,
you shall receive it.

And if my peace pipe is bad,
I'll personally flush it down—

cleansing my head
so I won't intoxicate
anyone with a bribe.

I move, swirling
to give off good vibes
that at my best, I prescribe.

Even while am sleeping,
I'm in touch with my tribe.

When I'm vibrating,
radiating good vibes,
I am the snake
everybody wants to be around.

I have drained
all my venom
to coexist with all of life,
so you can subscribe.

Same Day, Just a Different Beauty

My soul should be as light as my silk pants,
my flesh warm as woolskin,
my heart as big as my power animals,
my brain fresh as mint,
my bone structural as metal
and flexible like the tail of a fish.

I hope my blood
moves like healthy rivers
and not dry streams.
I let life be my teacher,
not a routine
read from books
we let dust consume.
I silence the fool in me
to become a dictionary of new experiences.
I laugh my way through life,
putting a stop sign to the serious and stiff
because my soul should be light.

As my flesh changes like real leather,
my brain watches
what my eyes see.
What a beautiful movie
I am living in!
Every day is a gift.
We can spoil it with our absence
or live it with gratitude
even if, even if...

More Affectionate

Let's be more human
and less digitally affectionate.

Is the world losing its true self
behind glasses of men?

Can we kiss, hug, and talk,
charging the light that darkness
seems to squeeze with wires missing human veins?

Let's make a true change
and bond as we did
when we depended on our parents' sweat.

Let's kiss, hug, and change.
Let's rewrap ourselves with the minerals
that God made us with.

Let your medicine release my medicine
and sneeze out tension
from this caption blinding our affection.

Let's kiss, hug, and change.
Let's laugh at our desires and pull down
our dreams from the realm of competition.

Let's return to the sideline of peace,
where our hearts
spark a new sense of affection.

Let's kiss, hug, and change.
Let's give up our flesh and be compassionate
to some one's aching soul.

Let's kiss, hug, and change.
Technology is inconsiderate to your lifespan,
so be more considerate with the time you don't really have.

Let's kiss, hug, and change.
Let's be advocates of something that makes us get off our bed
and throw away friendships that aren't meant to last.

Let's, kiss, hug, and change
corporate with the visions of God
and our inner dreams that find a nest to bask.

Let's kiss, hug, and change.
Let's illuminate the impossible
and believe in a new tomorrow
to be today's favorite memory.

Let's kiss, hug, and change,
allowing sincerity, playfulness,
love, and purpose
change the climate of our presence.

Fight to Be PRESENT

Everyone was born with wings to fly.
We must find the feather
that gives us the will
to attempt the dive.

Time goes by,
and the years say hi.
I don't have memories
of yesterday, just a
photograph from today.

Time goes by,
and the years say hi.
I wonder...
How far, how close
am I to my shaman?

Time goes by,
and the years say hi.
The clock keeps ticking
as our coach keeps meditating.
Things hardly change externally,
but within us, there's a world branching out.

Time goes bye,
and the years say hi.
What escapes from the cage
never returns.
The buildings are growing in the cities
like mountains in the field.

Time goes by,
and the years say hi.
We spent a quick blip on the earth,
having the power to slow down
and realize we should
not change the world
But fight to be present in it.

Time goes by,
and the years say hi
the same way
the new day returns
and we didn't
take advantage
of opening the gift
with a smile.

Faith

Faith is stronger
when we are in
bad positions.

Faith become weakened
when we are in
good positions.

Faith is more powerful
when we practice
in both conditions
good, bad
at peace.

Close Exhibition

I crave the freedom
zoo animals seek who tire from exhibition,
escaping thin wires and concrete vinyl.

I am the angel fish that circles around in a container of water,
seeking to retreat to the sunrise.
above the ocean.

I'm a cardinal
breaking away from the cage that overwhelms my wings.
I am rescued by my courage.

I am the fruit peels
that return to the field
to feed the earth my freedom.

I was once a life encaged,
and today I am freedom outside of that chaos.

Passing through the eyes of my fear,
I break away judgments of your uncertainties,
slowly returning to my true center
outside of your exhibition.

Changing Patterns

Warrior of the morning,
warrior of the night,
moving with a purpose
and you know why...

Warrior of the city,
warrior of the forest,
overcoming city challenges the size of trees
and climbing trees the size of buildings.

Warrior of the street,
warrior of the earth,
you know your environment
because you have walked on this earth before.

Warrior of the earth,
warrior of the sky,
you have conversations with mom and dad
to balance out your yin and yang.

Warrior who cries,
warrior who laughs—
Both feelings feed your soul.
So when you die,
they can't never say you didn't laugh or cry.

Warrior who has taken a stand,
warrior who hasn't taken a stand,
commit to yourself to humanizing
the earth that's missing hugs
that flower vines of peace.

Warrior carrying wounds,
warrior carrying joy,
pray to spirit
and wash away these feelings that cling
to the mind, oppressing the body
from experiences unlived by your spirit.

Ask Yourself

In a world with an answer
for every question,
how do I ask the questions
that are the most important in my life?

How do I get the answer
when I want to see,
but God closes me off and makes me wait?

In such a little world
with so much abundance of beauty,
how do I get to understand it all?

By getting lost in the smallest thing in this world,
I'll understand the biggest part!

In a world with so much inspiration,
why do I stay home feeling so bored?
Instead, perhaps I should paint the song
that I will dance to.

In a world with so many beautiful people,
why do I hide my uniqueness,
wasting the opportunity to undress
my eccentricity?

In a world of so much criticism,
why don't I act differently?
I need to escape from the rim of the parrot's beak,
set myself free, and start complimenting.

In a world so open,
why don't I find the nest of my spirit
to always have a refuge to recharge my creativity?

In such a beautiful world,
why do I let myself be carried away
by streams of clogged minds?

With so many examples of beauty all over the earth,
I used to choose the path of the conditioned...

Well, now I prefer to fly with a few good people
than crawl with an abundance of soulless people.

A Curious Soul

Why is it that
the leaves of the trees
separate from their branches
and with that separation,
they die, disconnecting
themselves from the cord, the veins
from the heart of the air
that sustains our life?

Why is it that
after being born, a turtle
takes its first step,
running to the sea,
not knowing the danger
that's outside its nest,
motherless and vulnerable in a whole world
of sand that should be giving us comfort?

Why is it that
love hurts when it leaves,
and when a new love returns,
we feel as if love never hurt before?

Why is it that
love erases our symptoms,
unstitching our skin open
with a new way of believing in love again?

It's like the moon
that shines in my sky for a while
and then rests
on other side of the world,
leaving my eyes sad
looking for the moon
that illuminates my sight,
but she always returns
when her stars begin to cry.

Life Is Way Too Beautiful

Life is way too beautiful,
so don't get stuck
on the beauty of one place.

Fly away with the wings
that are ready to take you away.
Don't limit your excavation
to the devil that invented segregation.

The earth didn't create borders;
the devil broke us apart
to make us feel stuck.

Who clipped your wings?
The world awaits
the landing of your feet.

We are like composers,
mixing in the garden of our communities
and discovering and admiring
the beauty in each other's dreams.

Let your heart be the pilot
of all the trips you take
and let your dreams fly away.

Become the passenger of faith;
The womb isn't the only egg we had to break.
Can you weave a today that meditates?

Isn't this a beautiful place?
We must prune what's toxic
and let good fruits pave the way.

Don't let dues make your movie a horror scene.
Prove yourself wrong,
and make things suitable for you.

See beyond your ache—
that you are shining truth
and walking in happiness as life become playful.

Life is not a field of condemnation.
Even though people walk in sinful thought,
be what makes anxiety delusional
to give God a meaningful point.

Beauty designs us
to share inches of love.
Don't be untruthful to the feelings in you
that want to be reusable.

Share what it feels to have
A bellyful of the beauty of life
so we all can ignite out of the usual.

I'm Here for You Today

The present is more stable than
a promising future.
I live for today to give my principles
a parent to look up to.

The present is more reliable
than a future fixed with agreements.
I open my eyes with the eyes of the sun
letting the fragrance of my chai with extra bergamot
open the nostrils of the sky.
I'm obligated to live today
because tomorrow is not guaranteed

The present condemns no one; she'd rather set you free!
Tomorrow can be a cell and yesterday, an open case,
if you don't liberate all your love in today to be yourself.

I am today's winner, even if I lose your expectation of me.
I prefer to give you a thousand kisses today,
than promise you a date tomorrow without me in it.

— GOD IS MY SHAMAN —

The Airport of Light

The light has arrived.
to erase your solitude
Here has come the light
so you feel its force!

There came the light
to put aside the fight.

There came the light.
to make the rest of the world triumph.
There came the light.
to erase the abuse.

There came the light.
to replenish the love
we've forgotten to drink from.

There came the light
to feel the good in you.

There came the light
to feel your presence.

There came the light
to sweep away anything
that isn't conducive to peace.

There came the light.
to create a new sight

There came the light,
switching to new insight.

There came the light
to repeat after you
all the desire that escapes from you.

There came the light,
squeezing out unremembered venom from a snake bite.

There came the light
to anchor the soil of your body with sunlight.

There came the light
to unite you with what
you have forgotten to love.

There came the light
when the satellite didn't respond to your SOS sign.

There came the light,
and no one was able to measure it in Fahrenheit.

There came the light
to protect your dream
and publish the sweat of a harmless dreamer.

There came the light,
and no one could blow out the candlelight.

There came the light
with an appetite healthier than all diets.

There came the light
with no favorite chosen land.

There came the light
to remind me that everything is alright.

There came the light.
like the silence in overnight jobs.

There came the light,
brighter than its goodbye.

There came the light
so you might accept growth as change.

There came the light
so you end the fight.

There came the light,
quiet like the footsteps of insects.

There came the light.
so you write about the experience
for the rest of your life.

There came the light
with a newborn's bite
and the attitude of new parents.

There came the light
to light up galaxies and awaken planets
to help me forget yesterday was dark,

accessorizing my body with hope,
reincarnating dreams I had
becoming the lamp of my soul.

May this be a reminder
that getting lost is how you can find yourself.
Make it remind you that you're alive
because stars await your rise.

The light borrows you and doesn't return you back
because the light understands
the importance of your luminosity.
And there comes the light
to feel its own serenity again.

Spiritual Seams

External needs and internal needs
are two different things.
Physical and spiritual:
tree skins and inner rings.
Physical and spiritual,
feeding the soul and the flesh.

Let me erase myself
so I can see what you need me to see within you.
Let me wipe the sweat off my body.
While you detoxify me, I'll sit by you
Transform me inside and out.

External needs and internal needs
are two different things.
Physical and spiritual,
feeding the soul and the flesh.
Glass loves the surface
and light fights to be contained
by its protective glory.

Let me dive into your being while you always rest in me
so I can get a feel of what my true needs are.
Swim on the surface of my inner body
so I can understand the construction of my canvas
while you decorate your flesh all divine
out of my fabric.

External needs and internal needs
are two different things.
Everyone sees the shiny button but not

everyone see what it takes to keep its peace
tame on top of bumpy fabric.

I can hear you in the darkness
of this night as I reach you in entrancing meditation.
I believe in capturing the brush that got lost in the spirit world
so I'll be able to see you
as the sun sees the moon before he steps into the light.
I step into you, not waving goodbye,
but I'll be back...

External needs and internal needs
are two different things.
Physical and spiritual,
feeding the soul and the flesh.

Tape my mouth, tape my comments.
Tape my words so I can be still
and hear you express yourself
without interrupting my shaman,
all while you have the mic in your hands
so later on, you can
un-tape everything you just stuck on me
so I can see physically and put together
what you have been trying to express
after I quiet my mind and give you
the chance to breathe on me.
I have a new pair of eyewear no stores have in stock,
seeing and understanding
my true inner and external needs.

Slow Growth

I am the roots of your dreams.
Come closer to me
with the water that runs from your fingertip.

I am the roots of your dreams.
When you're walking,
I am on the soles of your feet
giving you the strength to keep tap dancing.

I am the roots of your dreams.
Do not forget
to talk to me.
Here will be your advice
until the end of all your beginnings...

I am the roots of your dreams.
Treat me with love,
and you will see your dreams grow
with the same love that you gave me.

I am the roots of your dreams,
connected to you
like people to televised novels.

I am the roots of your dreams.
Sing to me all your songs,
and I'll make a Grammy from your devotion.

I am the roots of your dreams.
Can't you see you'll always
be a child dependent on me?

I am the roots of your dreams.
Give me your sweat and prayers as an offering.
I'll return to visions of peace
and mold them into your reality.

I am the roots of your dreams.
Weave your mind, body, and spirit
towards the light you seek.

I am the roots of your dreams.
Don't look in the hardware store,
addictions, or religious walls to greet me.
I'm in the entrance of your entire being.

I am the roots of your dreams.
Unfold like a lotus
so I can posses you with the love
of a gardener with no other needs.

I am the roots of your dreams.
Let me be the garment
that covers your patches and seams.

I am the root of your dreams.
Don't drain me with material prayer.
Excite me with your spiritual needs,
and I'll water your dreams
a centimeter by its root.

Old Soul

I'm a deep person.
I don't know
anything of the surface.
I'm a deep person.
I respect the essence
of everything.
I am not one to judge how the light is
installed on someone else's platform.

I don't look at things from the outside
because the inside
has way more to share with me.
I ask questions
that take me to deeper places.
I give responses that paint poems of understanding
from a deep place with deeper perspective,
breathing love above and under the sea.
I always find a way to be rescued by the rainbow.

I'm a deep person.
I'm not sorry for been weird
because this is who I am.
I am a great spirit by design,
and that's all the reassurance
I need to be myself:
deep like the stomach of a whale,
deep like my African lineage,
deep like a hollow tree.
I have a depth that no submarine can reach.
I'm deep like the path of a true mystic,

deep like the butterfly that can't find its caterpillar skin.
I'm deeper than any scientific research,
deeper than rocks and machines,
deep like old book covers with empty pages.
I'm so deep that I'm okay being alone,
that I can see when there's evil hate on a holy attempt.
I'm deep enough to understand how angry and calm waves /
can coexist,
deep enough to know that I can travel to God's heart
without needing to perish and resurrect.

With ink and the honesty of my heart,
I can transport
because I'm am an old soul.
I walk with a cane full of wisdom.
My skin holds no wrinkles yet,
just phrases that take you down faces that know better than.

Look into a turtle shell and get lost within
the story of life.
Hide within a snail home,
and you'll have to learn how to find the light.

I'm deep, but you make me abstract.
I'm in love with the seam that embroiders simplicity.
I wasn't brought to Earth
to be a scavenger of manmade problems.
I'm a lover of wisdom and serenity.
I dance on a floor that doesn't tremble.
Only God's roar scare me!

Being human is a test.
Being alive is an exam.
If you're no longer alive, you can't play the game
Being attracted to it was wise, not right.

I can have long conversations with willow trees.
I love sitting there
and listening to every echo, to every branch moving
like they're dying to be heard and hug my kind hands.
Some people can embrace my quiet moments
while others feel uncomfortable in peace.
My bones are made of stories, struggle, and glory.
I'd rather touch all life through my eyes
and not have lenses on or a phone.
I am a library full of books untouched.
I am an old soul.

Life Is a Classroom

Life gives lessons of unending chapters.
Life explains that the good could also be bad.
Life demonstrates that the bad is as educational as the good.
Life coaches us in how to interpret the playbook.
Life advises us that by judging, we only learn about our /
hidden scars.
Life opens eyes with every breath taken.
Life shows us that joyful people can be unattached yet
still grateful.
Life enlightens our place of peace.
Life professes that behind every mountain, something /
new stands.

Life will always be open for us,
as long as we are open
to its mysterious teachings.

Life begins when we stop controlling her.
Life knows every comet that passes through the sky.
Life turns the page that we don't turn for ourselves.
Life is a playground with too many grownups.
Life doesn't recognize a rewind button.

Life is a garden made out of glass that's fragile yet beautiful.
Life is crutch to its creator and available to its creation.
Life can be a dance-hall or a tatted jail-wall.
Life is a pure awakened smile.
Life is full of mistakes but still perfect in the moment.
Life cries for us
so we have essence to drink from.
Life wants of you the same for all,
for us to not skip class in nonsense.

Life is a marathon of who can be the most present.
Life is a short series we can make feel longer.
As we live outside, we become the Church of the /
Multipurposed.
Life is easier when we are less tired and more thankful.
Life is a chatroom for love and a recycle bin for hate.
Life is the playbook of birth and the event planner of death.
Life is a spiritual journey if you exercise the soul with /
reciprocal purpose.

Life is unfair to no one; it believes stars reflect on every soul.
Life knows every one's steps
just like God knows every one's organs.
Life needs us to retake the quiz
that we don't have to pass or fail.
Just live out of love!

Dancing Away

Alive, I enjoy
the dance that makes me forget my problems.
I give the presence my sweat
to feel present.

Staying away from earthquake
that hates the imagination of happiness,
my mind screams out flamenco,
my body swings out merengue,
and my soul hammocks out the day with reggae.
I sit down with Icaros, using my brain as a canvas.

I'm materialistically out of rhythm
but spiritually in tune with the Great Spirit.
I know because when we dance,
no one steps on my lazy feet.

Your Peace Is Always Tested

Follow the natural laws of the environment
so that you don't die on the date that you write
but on the day God has written for you.

Greedy fish die without knowing
they swam in water.
Wise fish die empty
but experience the entire ocean.

Your steps guide younger steps,
so don't dirty life, pick up your mess,
and be someone's living hero.

The current is free.
Don't try to control your entire life.
Fall sometimes and feel the sand.
Find your place of understanding on that beach.

Don't chase what shines.
It's better to find your own reflection
and there, you'll shine.

Escape from the shell
human beings gave to you
and find the one that God left for you
without intentions of shampooing and conditioning you.

Borrow clouds from the sky
and lie on top of them trusting
that sometimes, transparency has solid sides.
With faith, you'll fall differently.

Try to hug a shell
without thinking
of taking her pearls away.

Don't feel bad.
Remember, everyone picks on the tree
that has the most fruits.
Continue to be fruitful.

If anger is lava,
I'll take her on a dive into water
to discover the foundation
of love, calming down her eruption.

Stress and distraction
are an amputated soul,
seeking to take the place where you
seek hope and serenity.

It's wiser to be godly
and calmer daily
than bait in a pack of greyhounds.
Let holiness adopt your beauty
to give existence a home to play.
Devotional treasury.

Hardships run loose,
but you are contained by the home of peacefulness
in this field of earth you walk upon.
Great spirit prunes
the hunger of bullies,
and water is kind seeds.

Silence loves to be tested by ignorance.
Meditation doesn't compete with anything,
and free-styling prayers makes the soul
align with the body's footsteps on this earth.

Bears can hibernate
but humans have no choice but to protect
the tranquility of their mindset
from the hamster ball
they no longer wish to roll in.

You Want to Feel Light?

To feel light on this earth,
I let the sun
burn away
this God-given flesh,
carrying all my unwanted desires
and all its pain—
a drag race that burns happiness,
stealing the engine of my heart from aliveness.

To feel light on this earth,
I light up with the moon
to disappear with the night,
hiding behind every star
that decorates a mannequin sky
and resting my mind
within the soul
that brings our lands life.

To feel light on this earth,
I turn into a feather and fly,
breezing through the earth uncontrolled,
consumed by the winds
lost in their drama
till I'm tossed into a landscape
that makes me feel like I'm in an empty theater,
where new things can always begin again.

To feel light on this earth,
I float atop water like a frog,
paddling my way through

the surface of life
till I reach
the core
of this world
in my lightest point.

I shed my feathers!
I am no longer the battery,
the case, or the phone—
I learn to let go
and become spiritual light.

Yesterday Misses Me

I thank yesterday for letting me be;
I am grateful for the space
today gives me for expressing myself.
I'm all about today
as I let my old skin shed.
I give my old ways jealousy
as I take my new ways on a date.
When I used to walk soullessly, I felt pain.

Today, I find light to nourish,
and now I only feel the sting.
God whispers in my ears:
It's okay to burn your old skin,
even when it still fits the seam of your beauty.

I give my past roses
because it now lives in a cemetery.
I don't miss it;
I used to be a mixture of fruits that didn't
blend into anything fruitful.

Today, my presence smells
like chopped basil and peppermint.
I've never been the type to loose myself in psychedelics.
My highness always came when I closed my eyes.
I have taken time to question spirituality
outside the norms
and have chosen to find God
outside a cage—no one can encage in walls!

I used to cover myself in old skin.
I let every day pass me by
like a lazy kid covers himself under dirty bedsheets
till he starts smelling his own stink
and decides to clean those dirty sheets,
step outside his laziness,
and finally see the world he has been hiding from
for so long under his old skin
and those sheets that deceive him.
He was killing his chance
of being someone new every day...

Words

Ugly words don't exist
in God's dictionary.

Ugly words don't exist;
Dispirited people behind them do.

The ugliness exists when
we turn away from God's nature
of what life is simply about.

The ugliness is drawn by a liar
who promotes
a dictionary without beauty
and loses at the end of trading words
to the irresistible beauty of truth
that changes all misguided minds
who are willing to toss their hearts
into the pages of the divine
that lives in all of us—
a beauty that is not plastic.

The Mic

I have fallen
like my friend once fell.
I have abused beauty
that no longer belongs in my digestive system.

I have fallen in love with solitude
and know I am sensitive to loudness.
Walking outside the green zone,
anxiety attacks my soul.

Sometimes, peace can be a weight
I can't carry for too long.
It is challenged by the discharge of dissatisfied souls
and disturbed by manmade laws.

I must transport myself again
into the landscape of God's heart
and imagine the entire earth as a green yoga mat,
charging my entire being as my eyes close and music paints.

I'll then mediate and fall in love
with the mic that hears my prayers
and sings back the songs of peace.

The First Shaman

Tired
but still standing,
my hands are put together,
so I'm still working on myself.

Achieving my dreams
and slowly harnessing fear,
sleep is my rest.

To be alive
is the greatest blessing in life.
Foreign work doesn't challenge me.

Breathing in the air of this day,
I find my peace.
Walking in meditation, I observe with the air.

A servant of God,
I am full of life,
so I cry in tears of love.

Happiness lives in this sacred body,
and I have a wife
with a belly full of dreams.

She advises and feeds me;
We are a part of the same tree.
She's not going to let no one burn my rings!

I have been raised
by God
as a self-made shaman
till life and death takes me
to the spirit realm, infinitely.

SPIRIT

Spirit, cover me with your light.
Spirit, feed me with your current.
Spirit, inject me with your wisdom.
Spirit, teach me to walk in your footsteps.
Spirit, help me fit in your wardrobe.
Spirit, open my heart,
exploiting it
with your love.

Spirit, protect me from foreign weapons.
Spirit, teach me to hunt for what I need
and dismiss what I want.
Spirit, I am a guardian of your love.
Spirit, will I come to your light—
or is your light the sensation I already feel meditating?

Spirit, will I see you in my death as I saw you on my birthdate?
Spirit, you are the passion sweating out of my visions.
Spirit, you are the light, shadow, and mystery.
Spirit, you are the magic schooling miracles.

I am learning to live
life as your dependent
without regrets.

Shedding Hair

As we get closer to death,
we stress less and laugh more.
As we get closer to our last meditations,
we get wiser and less rebellious.
As we get closer to the big question,
our view of life opens up
like a woman giving birth
and a man's life alongside his wife takes on a new form.
As we get closer to the falling tree,
Great Spirit prepares our nest.
As we get closer to our last sorrows,
we appreciate bad people
and love good people deeper.

As we get closer to death,
the sun consumes our light
and the moon consumes the shine of our sadness.
As we get closer to the symphony of the earth,
we start smelling the grass for what she is
and not as what we spray her to be.

As we get closer to our last spiraling dance,
the sky and the earth
unite worlds and become one being.
As we get closer to realization,
we see that eternity doesn't come in the flesh.
Instead, it comes in the flesh of Spirit
embarking on countless journeys.
As we get closer to our true fear,
our visions of faith get clearer than

all philosophical and religious texts.
As we get closer to our lightest tears,
we'll notice we're just here
to reconvene with some good and bad friends.

As we get closer to God,
we start accepting that our lives
has always been
a colleague under construction.

Shedding for the Good

Shed till there is
no more to thread,
to be at a level of consciousness
where you no longer
exist in heavy flesh.

Shed till there is
no more to be said,
so the stress
weighting your head down
falls apart into pieces of scales.

Shed till there is
no more swirls ahead
that cost you pain,
so you walk in trails
you paint with unbroken brushes.

Shed till there is
no more to shed,
to be left with a heart
that bumps to the beat of life,
skinless from attachment
that causes the heart to enlarge.

Shed till there is
no more to shed,
reaching godheads
to be free from form
and at last, be free from
those parts of you that no longer
sprout fruits.

Peace over Reaction

When evil is present
put on God's repellent
and remember why we meditate.

When evil is loose,
find the most solid part in you
and join with the most tender stone.

When evil is loose,
don't lose faith.
Look at the direction of God.
Inside you, there's a heart.
Manifest it to the one who has no rhythm of love.

When evil takes a bite out of you,
do not give it tears.
Keep them stored for the river
that is drying up.

When you feel the pressure of evil,
look to the sky and the earth.
Notice what you see in front of you:
We are a print on a never-ending fabric.

Don't let the empty art galleries
that others don't want to self-correct
destroy the color of your peace.

Our Potential

Everything in this world
has a heart,
and the ones who don't recognize it
don't know what love is.

Like the moon and the sun
from night to day, they adore each other
without making a noise
to not destroy what lights up our day.

Like a squirrel claiming a tree as home,
marking the entrance with its morning chirping song
freezing nuts aside ancient roots,
surviving with what it knows.

Like rivers and sand
trade off massages
inside every breeze
that crosses their bodies.

Like humans fall in love,
giving new tribes new markings
to identify the evolution of geometry.

Everything in this world
has a heart,
and the ones who don't recognize it
don't know what love is.

Like a Taino loves his arrows,
because as he grows, his bow sharpens his faith.

Like a Taina loves her land,
because the land teaches her how to mother.

The earth loves you, my son , but the world challenges you.
Acknowledge the roses that God offers you.
It is never too late to be born again.
Change in growth
and forget who you were before.

Everything in this world
has a heart,
and the one who doesn't recognize it
doesn't know what love is—
a closet full of stories,
a woman desiring more breasts,
a father requesting more strength.

Love sparks the beginning.
God seals the deal
and you write in the gaps
if love chooses you as its possession.

I'd rather see the world
with a child's eyes
that has just fallen in love for the first time
or has had their heart broken many times—
nonetheless grateful that love has visited me numerous times.

Everything in this world
has a heart,
and the one who doesn't recognize it
doesn't know what love is.

My Train Ride

Morning prayers on the train
calm my nerves into grains of peace.
Morning prayers on the train
calm humanity's chest pain.

Morning prayers on the train...
yet I am not awake.
If I don't, I exchange some words with God.
Morning prayers on the train
erase nightmares,
turning my morning into the sweetest of dreams.

Morning prayers on the train
make me greet the person next to me,
making the homeless think I am insane
because I believe in change.

Morning prayers on the train...
yet I am not awake
until I have a cup of tea with God.

Morning prayers on the train...
I hear the tracks whisper to me—
that we are all passengers on Great Spirit's back.

Morning prayers on the train
protect me from evil eyes
flying around unhappy minds.

Morning prayers on the train...
yet I am not awake
till I am naked and grateful
in front of God's yoga mat.

Morning prayers on the train...
I hear the horn shout out.
My responsibilities give birth to my intentions.
My intentions teach me how to be responsible.
Responsibility nurtures my dreams.
Dreams hold my art:
poems full of prayers.

Great spirit reminds me
that we are all working souls,
representing the light
that emanates from a great spirit
into the rail that rides our prayers.

Morning prayers on the train...
There is an ache in the eyes
of the ones who don't feast
on divine light.

Morning prayers on the train...
I am a baby rock
by the flow of this electrical wagon.

Morning prayers on the train...
I am a lighting bug
inside the intestines of Mother Earth.

Morning prayers on the train...
I trust my growth as I practice
swapping out my heart for love.

Morning prayers on the train
close the door on negativity,
riding stars underground.

Morning Sky

What a beautiful surface!
Heavenly father, carry me on your
shoulders so I can breathe as you breathe.

What a beautiful giant
opening like the heart
of the earth!

What a beautiful bottle top!
I can see you unwrapping
freedom.

What a marvelous ceiling!
You send us winds to
trail us to you.

What a beautiful headwrap
that cries tears
on dry days to feed the fruits of life!

What a brand new duvet cover!
How nice is it to walk in the morning
and feel like the mattress of a new horizon.

Charged by the sun and charge me
with all your energy
so we grow as you invite spring.

Just Let It Burn

Ima beg this fire
to help me burn my past,
burying the damage that yesterday
unconsciously marked on someone's existence.

I will arouse this fire
so I transform into a healthy dish
as I share my prayers next to this candle
that sees the attempt at my growth.

I will persuade this fire
to clean my wounds
and remind me of my missteps
so whenever they want to take me
on a dance again, I'll know best.

I will fan this fire
to melt me into the pot where
vegetables and meat mix to create a hearty soup,
sweating so I value the time cooking under the sun.

I will call upon this fire
to burn all the spirits that railed me down
the hill of dimness once, and now that
I have learned to fight negative influences,
I'll blow them away like ashes
without needing violence.

Basement Breaks

I smoke this tobacco
to exhale the secrets
of the land native to its stem.

I hold this tobacco
as if I was romanticizing
the stem of a rose.

I read the veins of this tobacco
to understand what it is
that am inhaling.

I treat this tobacco
the same way my ancestors gently roll
their fingers on its soul.

I have the same destiny as tobacco.
God smokes me as I disappear in
life's ups and downs.

One day, I will be someone's tobacco
as I swirl like smoke
in the sky and the earth.

Like this smoke escapes from
the opening of my mouth
into the unknown,

I trust that every day,
I am getting closer to the bud
of the Great Shaman's heart:
God.

I Can't Be Your Best Friend

I'll fight the devil
with the swords of Spain.
I'll fight the devil
with Japanese blades.

I'll fight the devil
with the knife grandpa sliced oranges with.
I'll fight the devil
with my grandmother's cane.

I'll fight the devil
so I won't stumble on the wrong path
and instead maintain my imperfection
by my humility.

I'll fight the devil
like dogs and cats.
I'll fight the devil
to keep my footprints on sacred paths.

I'll tell the devil
during meditation
to not enter here
with emptiness
because I'm full of life,
as I see life
with the eyes of a shaman.

GOD of Your Earth

God hides in a mountain,
God paints in a cave,
God dances in a river,
God rests in a belly,
God sleeps in the mind.

You don't have to go too far to consult it,
nor look for a man to cry.

Do you know how to talk to its spirit
and search where no one can enter?

There God will be,
meditating in the earth
of your body
where only you can enter.

Carry Away

Let the river convey me.
I trust her current
and have given myself
to the spirit
who sleeps and flies
in nature.

Lift me, raven,
to the basement of Heaven.
I am not afraid.
Yesterday, I prepared for the flight,
and today my wings are anxious
to be brushed by the winds.

Relocate me, hurricane.
Shift me with the force of these winds.
I'll find ways to unbuckle the fears of my body,
landing on Earth with new a form of bravery.

I'll let go like Caribbean green butterflies
in this land
full of hidden surprises.

Transfer me, ocean.
Transplant me, Love.
I'm a student of freedom.
I listened to my teacher Nature
in this land, teaching awareness.

Letting myself go, I'll transform!
Without fear, I'll find The Beyond
I could have not dreamt of alone.

Because all I had to do
was ask my spiritual designer
about liberty.

Call

Let the spirits arrive
without knocking doors,
sweeping all malignant
hidden forces.

Let the drum scream,
knocking down the leaves
of the demons running loose
in the landscape of your form.

Pass the microphone to some maracas
and let them sing a song of joy.
Now a body moves:
leaps and jumps.

Accept the time.
God clocks in to cleanse your heart,
lighting you up like incense.
You move in a new spiritual form.

Receive blessings that never stop.
Thank Spirit
that created all that is sacred,
including the waters that
cleanse all the corners of your home.

Call upon the Light

Light that is getting closer,
knock me down like you knocked down
the ego of a rooster.

I will find the power
of each animal you weave
while my eyes are aware and hypnotized.

You arrive in everyone that thinks
they have no fault
to light up the landscape
of the bumps on the sea floor.

I'm opening the tunnel of my body
for you to enter with your speed
along the highway of my veins
the same way you converted
the city and the countryside into a circus
that does not shut down.

I don't need a lens to see you
or special glasses to protect my perception of you.
I am dressed by the same light
you illuminate in me.

Now I shine
like the countryside and the city.
Who lives in your divine light?

When I Was a Devil

I believe in forgetting and forgiving
just like fresh paint can form
new wombs out of jubilant umbilical cords.
That's why I receive the Devil with a hug
if it comes to me again
so that all its grudge go away.

I'll receive the Devil with a plate of food
if it comes to me one more time
so you can see that there is no separation at this table.

I'll receive the Devil with my hands
if it comes to me in multiples
for you to see that there are friends
who emerge and sow light into your life.

I'll receive the Devil and I talk to it about love
if it comes to me in twos—
not to change its religion
but to feel its heart.

I know they speak ill of you,
but I know there's someone sweet behind you.
You are a butterfly behind a cocoon of fire.
When your lack of love turns off,
you will cook a new you,
because it's never too late
to kill and forget your wrongdoings from the past.
Let's give the good side in us all a chance
to turn a devil into a god.

When I was a devil, I walked with broken yins and yangs
while questioning God's existence.
No one cared about me
'cause I didn't have love to give.
Pickpocketing was my sport
and big sales Super Bowl.

I was known as a delinquent.
I cut my own wings.
I had no spiritual guide lifting me.
I enclosed myself in a cage
that only complimented my misdeeds.
I didn't know anything about spirituality.
I robbed from my parents and left students without laptops.
I walked on a field of thorns
and didn't believe roses could grow out of their own thorn.
I led a gang of street bacteria with a malignant laugh.
Everyone knew me by my painted lies,
and I walked with an erected mind.

When I was a devil, I ate from the plate
that didn't know true love.
When I was a devil, everyone hyped my bad deeds
and crushed the good ones that attempted to breathe.
When I was a devil,
the street gave me a nickname.
When I became wise,
God gave me purpose
as my new name.

Behind Every Mountain

Behind every mountain,
there's a gift for you
from Gaia—

Spirit of all, within all
creator of all gifts
that we forgot to see.

It doesn't matter
from where you start the climb.
All that matters is that you start now.

Climb it alone, and it'll take you longer to see the gift.
Climb it with the mystic all of mystics,
and you would learn to share the gift.

Climb with four legs.
Have faith
and not expectations.

The gift you seek is not an anchor on the tip.
Rather, on the other side,
the sun hit where
clarity paves the way.

Look at the view of this earth...
Gaia has made for all.
What do you truly desire
that won't take away from
the center of your peace?

— EXPERIENCING ONENESS —

My Guardians

We are all brothers and sisters.
Our last names play games.
The moon is our mother.
The sun is our father.
The earth is our nanny.
The spirit of God is
our true shelter.

Immigrants of Oneness

Visitors of a circus.
Fading balloons seeking the hands that anchor them.
A marching band full of life,
questioning human's highest potential.
We are naturally curious, which is why
we fall in love with everything our hearts demand,
seeking spiritual gain rather than economic oppression.
Emotional cannonball.
An individual seeking tribalism,
tribalists seeking freedom.
Question marks on the move,
costumes playing a role.
Souls seeking to direct their own roads.

We all have the option to be heroes.
Instead of determining the villains' role,
we all carry weapons that can pierce negativity,
shooting smiles from lips that
haven't forgotten their humor and minds,
that can be trained to be impenetrable.
Hearts spreading free love recharged by
the container that needs no one to carry its spirit.

We are aware that we are a warehouse full of dreams
and one hospital is filled with anxiety.
A church smiles while walking into raves.
Untamed children are hungry for more
with stomachs that God tickles.
We are the transaction of souls to souls,
sometimes lost and found in other body forms.

If God was a plane, we'd all be anxious riders.
Can we learn to trust like we fill heaven
while our eyes are filled with the inner world?

We are all parts of the same birthmark,
sentences that never end with moles.
We are the end of heavy historical tyranny.
I am enraged in love.
Without a choice, God is my Valentine.
Every day, I talk to myself,
making my ancestors dance.

We are the zone that fuels us to be better human beings.
I race when it comes to faith and meditate.
I stop when there is a debate or a war.
The first step I take out of bed
says thanks you, and the second, I trust you.
We are all immigrants to our desires,
native to oneness—
the property of life
and trophies of death.
Nobody or nothing can
oppress the best memory.
We are brothers and sisters
of oneness.

I Am Missing Something

Buttons are looking for a garment,
playing tug of war with the ego and self-liberation

We are God's art pieces
in Mother Earth's art gallery:

the glow of the moon,
the flares of the sun.

When life becomes my seamstress,
I turn into an experimental mannequin.
We are trims seeking the edge.

I paint molds of the inner divine to the ultimate form,
lanes that yield to the Tao.

Frogs leap on lilies, and I discover chakras,
divorcing outer satisfaction.

I get married to self-transformation,
giving self-balance a personal definition

bringing inner peace roses every day,
so she does not flee from my being.

I am learning to be the beats
that radiate from the drum of oneness.

Freckles of You

We are different tree rings
but the same leaves;
different prints but the same species;
fragile like snails
and parakeets.

We are different vehicles
but powered by the same engine;
different airports
but the same plane;

designs made by the same designer;
fragile like a womb.

We are not owners of houses,
nor landscape conquistadors.
We were born to sign the contract
of self-care and discovery in divine oneness.
We are mystical by nature
and shamanic by spiritual background.

I let my actions place me in debt with oneness,
popping my ignorance
with the curiosity of a child.
God is like a giraffe,
and we are all its patches.
We can't run away from
experiencing oneness.

Don't Be Absent

Let's hold hands and do what we love.
Clouds will form in each other's skies.
Turn into a ball and trust life as our QB.
Let's make boredom smile
so she finally marries someone and settles down.
Let oneness be my higher self
as I become the Velcro that finds
seams unbroken to rejoice with.

I fall in love with my past, present, and tomorrow
because life is too short to condemn yesterday,
and I was wrong for disrespecting today.
I give tomorrow the trophy the present deserves first.

I glorify the conscious
and I idolize the wise.
listening to the song
the divine cries for us daily
as the sun rises by our windows,
unlocking my soul
and turning me into a flying ballerina.

God pointed me out,
so I toss the ball to the rest of humanity.
In poems that cry
the emotion of love,
we should all march.
With smiles, rescue others
With kind unpredictable actions.

We should knock on each other's doorbells,
taking the moments from time.
We missed out
because love wants us all
to lay in a hammock
under the shade of thankfulness.

Can I make a pattern out of your
struggles to help you bloom?
Call me your brother or sister
without having to play a role,
giving Oneness the script to rip apart
as we love each other as siblings
of the one and only.

Pattern-Making

Stars looking for the moonlight;
flowers listening to the anthem of the morning;
students skipping class to meet up with a special girl;
a lost tribe searching for those obliterated tracks;
crows migrating on tours in the wind,
their ears on prey alert and looking for protection;
roots oppressed by the illusion of segregation.

We are the feathers linked to the Great Spirit's wings,
tail feathers expanding from the earth's horizon.
We are preyed on by systems and beliefs
that make us into pieces of a pattern
that are once again sewn together by the great one
and our personal hunger to feel the spoon
that satisfies our spiritual urges.

Braided Together

We are strands of a spider web
that make a new harp;
different fibers
forming a whole quilt;
triangular bands hugging billiard balls;
identical coins with different faces.

We are various flowers in one botanical garden;
the creeks of streams making the ocean;
the pain behind the smile that explodes happiness;
strokes of pleasure, making-up sex.

We are layers of glaze paint demonstrating one masterpiece;
the experience resulting of our actions;
our enlightenment's reflection;
the tear from many faces falling into the same bowl.

We are each other's napkins;
the intention that sneaks through the gap
between each other's teeth;
the sincerity that propels us forward.

We are at different coordinates
on the same map.
We are the oneness that makes
segregation visit
his therapist.

Seeking the Seeker

We are an empty prescription bottle
seeking divine medicine;
loose wheels seeking the holy body;
babies depending
on life's transporter
and messenger of oxygen;
the hands awaiting help;
the heart listening to a poem of self-love;
an instrument waiting to be played by someone;
art waiting to be touched;
a vintage shop hoping to not be forgotten;
a new phone with broken screen
preserves buttons from a different generation.

We are the prayer we sing.
We are what unfolds during meditation.
We are the reason God sends us to play.
We are kites gradually being returned
to the hand that built them.
We are the gossip between life and death.
We are the covers of our own book
and our actions are the chapters
that make us skip through life
in divine ways.

Oneness

Pause and chop down on all distractions.
Open your mouth and let's be relatable.
Reminder: God designed us so we don't feel alone.
Declutter your mind from the past.
Today, a vacuum of new experiences.
Hug me like you tap on that app.
I'll be the page waiting to be changed.
Look into the water of your nakedness,
and you'll remember what it felt like to be in the womb again.

We make music while we stomp on the earth.
If you feel like your life has been a lie,
take off the accessories that don't let you be naked.
We all seek truth—
truths that take us out of our comfort zone.

Are you ready to grow?
Like nature rises and puts us
to sleep season after season,
the DJ scratches the record,
and God makes our spirits spin.

Nothing makes me different.
Try to find the lie that doesn't exist,
and you won't be breathing from the same brush
that painted me in you and you in me.
We are all part of the same vision.

Life expands like anaconda skin
and is profound like every Amazon tree.

Burning sticks on a drum,
the world is formed.
We may be divided by oceans,
but we are united in the spirit of one forest.

Can we talk about the good news?
Perch like sparrows.
Break challenges with the teeth of squirrels.
Look at life as a reflection stored in all our organs.

If I'm not scared of myself,
I can't be scared of the world.
If I love myself,
I shouldn't be scared of...
discovering parts of me outside of me,
giving a new star to daily oneness,
buckling my adventure into a stroller behind wild parents,
calling the moon and the sun my guardians,
falling in love with every woman I see
but making love to one
that lifts and transplants my heart.

I'm scared to see what sleeps on the other side of the rainbow,
yet I'm curious to see where the colors guide my soul.
Make a mess out of my life, and call it spiritual abstraction.
We have been isolated from oneness for way to long.
The mother calls upon her child to return home,
where I recognize that we are all One, even if we don't act /
like it.

The Mother of Oneness

Look at the veins on your hands
and those veins on that leaf...
Feel the slim hair of a rose
and the hairs on your back that you can barely see.
Rub your hands on those rocks
and feel the dry wounds on your flesh.

Look into the eyes of animals
and find the reflection of your existence.
Look at how you shed hair,
like how fall turns into nakedness.

Leap through the jungle of oneness
like a newborn monkey.
Escape a kangaroo's pouch
and ask the divine question
that makes the mind shiver
when the heart begins to ask:

Do you like how the circle looks
when it invites other shapes
to dance along with its wholeness?

We are the coordinates
that rely on the same foundation .
Oneness speaks to everyone in alikeness.
We are the balance that doesn't lean to the left or right.
Oneness doesn't divide us with preference
because we are united by love.

We are bumper cars launched by the same machine.
We are highways affected by the same breeze.
We are subway maps organized in purpose.
We are pieces of Connect 4 depending on
the leap and climb of each other.

We are a garden groomed by an invisible spiritual botanist,
a lab constantly repairing its plan,
A gang of geese sketching out a map.

Rats survive thinking about the rest of the tribe.
Crows chant "God is the only caw you cannot silence."
We are dragonflies sharing the sky.
We are ants building empires.
We are an old game backed up with new rules.
We are the veins making oneness's heartbeat pump again.

— Respecting the Earth and Admiring the Skies —

The Cónuco

The Cónuco says:
Move your earth
for when you wake up,
so you can eat yucca, yams, and mango.

You won't feel sad
for your hunger
if you get up early,
greeting the sun,
and chant the song of thankfulness.

The Moon says:
Don't forget to say goodnight
because I'm the one who
watches over your sweat
while the lazy prefer to steal
from the work they don't put in.

Sensual and emotional
is the living being
who drives their sweat over the earth—

One with her changes
holy with nature,
and dependent on her magic.

The Cónuco says:
Sing me songs
and massage my body
with the softest part of your body.

Roll your soul over my walls
and gamble all your meditation
over my floor.

Don't hurt the flowers,
nor step over a stranger's dream
You don't know how long he
has been waiting to see
the sprout of his wounds.

Greet the sun,
talk to God,
and let the moon tuck you to sleep.

Create a facewash
out the herbs that hug your intestines
and learn to self-heal.

Plant your true dream
in an organic garden
and you see truth grow out of uncertainty.

Don't abandon the high of God
for the note of liquors
or a hit from crack.

If you get sick,
you can always find your home
in the garden of my remedies.

Cónuco is a plot of cultivated land, generally small. A conuco is a Taino
gardening practice.

Mother Love

The love of a mother
is like the ways
of a snail—
It sticks to you,
so you never forget her advice
while you set out on your journey
outside the nest.

The love of a mother
is like the song
of a rooster that never tires
until you learn the lessons
among her sayings.

The love of a mother
seizes and holds you
like the tree trunks
hold shaky hammocks.

A mother's love
caws like a rooster,
reminds me of snail trails,
and it is firm like a pine tree
branching out from ancient roots
on fresh new grass.

A mother's love
is even felt after burial.

A mother's love
is a poem that lacks a title
and has so ending.

A mother's love
sticks like a burn-mark
and grows like healed wound.

A mother's love
is an open basket
and a full fridge.

A mother's love
catches your fall on wet soil.

A mother's love
carries you all the way.

A mother's love has a stare
that can sentence you
for the rest of your life
with forgiveness,
compassion, and support.

A mother's love
becomes that punching bag
of hardship.

She would burn her forest for you.
She would get a master's degree in therapy
to help you understand your pain.

She is the best weaver of hugs that comfort
a skeleton departing from love.

She has a head with more than two ears,
sheltering ants with dry leaves

She rises the earth so her community doesn't flood.
She serves herbs and fruits,
so we take class when our body falls apart.

She gives us food as medicine and sheds roots,
ensuring that we are always eating
fresh and up-to-date nutrients.

She tests our stamina
in slopes with different textures.
She's a reflection of ourselves.

We are kids lost in a city
that miss the botanical wardrobe of the earth
and the reflection of the stars.

Bigger than Me

I am a miniature egg in your nest
the same way
I am an itsy bitsy fish
in your river.

I am a peewee turtle in your sand
the same way
that I am a microscopic raven in your sky.

I am a pint-sized giraffe on your farm
the same way
that I am a tiny squirrel in your tree.

I'm a little bean in your pot
the same way I am
life in your womb.

Oh, my giant globe!
Oh, my Mother Earth!
I'm just fall leaves
in your autumn,
screws seeking placement,
your toolbox,
baby hair on your forehead
erosion of a massive rock,
leaking paint from a tube
full of caves,
the mist of an upcoming storm,
the seed of the tree's fruit,
the footprint of your being ,

the water running through giant pipes,
an ant under shoulder pads
the blow of a whistle.

I'm the pigment of the holy shape,
nails massaging the earth,
scales naturally returning home.

I look into every lifeform's eyes
and see your glow
all around the earth.

With Her Permission

I would dig
in the land of my mother
to find the art that lives in her
and with that same art,
accept her beauty.

I'll ask for her permission
to design with the particles
that she sheds every season.

I'll spread the fantasy
that is hidden between her cherry blossom trees
and behind her pale pink petals.

With her permission,
I'll do the most honorable act on this earth
and catch her response through omens
while hearing mariachi over a castle porch.

Listening to the tune of her voice.
I get a chance to listen to life itself.
We all thought it was muted
when we moved from the countryside
to the city of metal and fighting cats.

With her permission,
I'll walk on earth with shattered glass
and not get cut.

I dig into my fears
and awaken to new wings.

I cut flowers to give my lady:
the roots of lilies and dandelions.

Her grass has turned into my hammock
and my hammock is an airplane
rocked by the breeze—
every bit of me.

I turn her wisdom
into a spiritual dictionary,
an inviting poem.

The moon and the sun
shines brightly in her lantern.

With her permission,
God dries his body after every shower.

I find the truth that bothers
what makes me ache.

My body is baptized,
my spirit is free,
and my mind is inspired.

Crows become an orchestra's conductor,
squirrels become rock bands,
doves become opera singers,
and insects become songwriters.

The trail is pruned for hikers.
Her floor becomes a bohemian's resting point
and her landscape is painter's new home.

Every instrument gets its tone,
every leaf gets its shape,
and every soul gets rewarded
with a taste of enlightenment.

WHY?

Sky, why are you crying
so many drops?

I cry to refresh the skin of the earth.

Why do so many plants grow out of you, Mother Earth?

I have millions of daughters to feed,
and I need to teach them to be brave so they can stand.

Why do you sing the same song, little sparrow?

Because I am the master of my gift,
and now I sing to you with my mastery
in a single song so you learn one day to be a master too.

Why do you eat so much trash, landfill?

Because humans do not stop at anything,
and it's my turn to eat the rest of their goodbyes
that are intoxicating my appetite.

Nature, why do you destroy us through natural disasters?

Because nothing gets your attention more than the death of /
a loved one,
so I detach you from the closest things you love
so you can see reality from the eyes of absence.

Why do you die, beauty in life?

Because there are more beautiful things
behind me, and if I don't die,
the beauty of my today would fade.
Because I have left my ego
stuck in yesterday…

The Clouds of Heaven

On a flight that I missed,
       I had the chance to see the clouds
              with a new ticket...

The sky is a floor full of clouds.
Heaven gives birth to layers of pillows
settled on top of each cloud.
Heaven is the graveyard of my ancestors.
The sky is the nest of God
and Heaven is an endless desert.
Heaven is another world based on my eyes.
For the spirits up here, heaven is a haven.
The sky is full of caves lost behind hidden clouds.

Heaven has its own great cannon.
Heaven is an active body lying on top of the earth.
Heaven looks like vanilla ice-cream decorated with /
blue sprinkles.
Heaven is the bed of the stars and the moon.
Heaven is the playground of birds and planes.

The sky is one of the greatest wonders of the world
drawn by greatness—
someone bigger than all the airports that travel in its clouds.
The sky is the driveway for these ancient and new clouds.
Heaven is the temple of clouds that practice meditation.
The sky is a stadium full of balloons tied to the earth,
bearing the weight and wonder of our existence.

The sky is so old that I see gray hair on its clouds
from the window of this plane.

From Orlando to Detroit to New York,
I feel the wonders of the sky clothing my mind
like a cotton sheet wraps the body that keeps
these poems of earth and sky alive.

Eternal Land

The land lives on.
The earth does not die.
The only one that dies here is me.

To not die guilty,
I will take care of this land
to continue the fight
of simply respecting
the freedom that she gives me.

I understand her secrets
as I'm alive on her grass
reading the pages of her body,
entering mountains,
traveling seas,
making love,
entering heaven.

Waking up with the sun,
I live present and cheerful
so that when my time comes,
it takes me slowly like a gleaming light.

Oh, great friends,
We must pass
'cause the sun desires
to shine over more newborns.

Spirit in me shines
like the sun over the beach
and as I get closer to light,
I shine with God.

Every day,
the spirit in me
gets warmer
as the sun heats
up the earth.

I can see that
life is part of death,
and death is a new entrance.

Don't Forget to Look at the Sky

Beautiful sky, open sky,
special sky, charming sky,
sky with senses, sky that is omnipresent…

I got lost in your clouds,
and you found me
finding you.

I rise in your first name,
so you give me your last.

You are never the same on the next cloud cap.
You are always revealing different parts of yourself.

Your clouds swim in your space
like turtles in a lake full of lilies.

Heavenly sky, I can always talk to you.
You answer with raindrops
and greet me with the hands of your clouds.

The sky covers the earth
and the earth covers me.
We are a triad.

Oh dear sky, the earth has always been
your first love, an unbroken marriage
that neither rocket-ship nor condor can break.

Your body is the reason;
I question the sun and moon.

Sky, your clouds are the softest hills
I have climbed
with my eyes filled with poetry.

Sky, you are the tent I had to learn
to have a relationship with.

You're the journal that feels
every line that escapes my heart.

You are the ceiling carrying
all the Hall of Fame stars.

You're clouds on pages describing the current.
Sky, you are the mailbox that holds all my prayers.

Blue and Green

God is a permanent shaman
and my Goddess is a healer of an aching body.

God, you are a rainbow rim circling around my head.
My Goddess, you are the roots raising my feet.

God massages my mind, so I think.
My Goddess gives me space within her body,
so I play with pigments that need lines to hug.

God, you shine like yesterday and like today.
You need no varnish, for you are the gloss stars seek.
My goddess, you always have space for me
under the room of your breast.

God taught me
that I must only fight peacefully
for what I truly feel in my heart
and abandon the rabbit that got lost in my head.

On the earth that everyone walks,
under the sky that few see above,
I speak to both divine mysteries
with no separation because
they're a marriage no one
yet seems to accept
between blue and green.

Be There for Me, Father, Like a Celestial Father

O Great Father,
you are up above,
watching down below,
protecting our mothers,
and training your children in multiple ways.

O Great Father,
your rain is nourishing,
drifting away our pain
in streams of soaked napkins
that love to swim in clearways.

O Great Father, your body is penetrable—
your hands, an open sky of lines,
and your presence,
a smile after a father sees his newborn stretch.

O Great Father, your sky is open for all.
Your clouds were made so
we can ride them to your heart
without needing a cardiologist referral.

O Great Father, you sometimes are misunderstood.
The fathers you send us leave us at an early age,
leaving our mothers alone.
Maybe that's the reason why
people don't look up at the sky anymore;
They have lost hope—
a hope that fades away when
fathers claim they would stay but leave,

when fathers abuse flowers in labor,
when fathers forget to hug their children
like the clouds hug us daily.

Dear men, dear father, let's take a stand
and put aside all seeds of distraction.
Let's be a conscious dream
where we meet our kids
like the moon and the sun take a trip.

Take Care the Earth

Who going to feed us
if we don't take care
the earth?

Are we going let the machines
take over and kill our mother,
burning hands of flowers
to now be fed by hands of butchers?

There is a disease rising
behind the screen we are all lost in.
Our purpose got lost in a home-screen button.

There are children dying of hunger,
so let's unzip the shade
and let the forest be our home.
How can we place a price on the Earth?
Does she charge us for our hunger
when God sends us bread to break?

Who going to feed us
if we don't take care the earth?
She is dying slowly.
Little by little,
she disappears
and her anxiety rises.

We are dreaming a reality
that doesn't relate to holiness,
planting seeds of fear indirectly.

We can now see
that we don't have to be fat or skinny
to be greedy and ambitious.
So instead, let's find the balance our spirit
and finally feel at ease.

Look at the yin!
Look at the yang!
Do they desire anything beyond their essence?

Let's understand balance and honor
our masculine and feminine decisions.
Let's learn to take care of the earth,
the playground
that we shall preserve
for the next cubs
of our tribes.

God's Heart

We are the arteries and veins
surrounding God's heart.
There are infinite ways to enter
the holy being...

Only if we don't consider
ourself
greater than
the pump
reviving us daily.

The mass can survive
without a vein,
but the veins can't breath
without the source.

Look at the leaves of a tree
and the pattern it breathes each season
that passes by...

Who can truly live
without being connected to the earth?

Love your nanny
and all the teachings
she imparts you with every time you fall on her skirt.

Trees die to give your body a home daily.
How can thankfulness not escape your tongue?

I respect people that work
and understand
the beginning of every source.

Factories and machines
block the soul
from understanding the process
that molds true beauty out of the earth.

We need a clean sky
and a mopped earth
to coexist in dimensions
that die to see more green jobs
growing out of a generation
screaming "save the world!"

God knows the craving of our dreams,
but if we are not at peace
with the ways of nature,
we can't plant a tree.

Pamper the creature of nature.
Place your ears on a tree trunk.
Rest your aching body on fresh grass,
and you'll meet your true provider.

Greaseless Bear

I have arrived,
bear of the mountain,
with this hunger to wander around,
looking for honey
in the trees, in the trash,
on the edge of the mountain,
and inside the heart of the forest.

I have arrived,
bear of the mountain,
with this hunger for stories saved by pigment,
looking for fish.
Where have the fish gone?
What happened while I was sleeping
in the cave of my ancestors?

I have arrived,
bear of the mountain.
With this hunger, I pray the suffering is worth the wait:
100 pounds less,
stomach cleanse.
This new sunlight
feeds my being with
new life, and spring calls for a change.

I have arrived,
bear of the mountain,
with this hunger to be a new being out of hibernation
once again stepping on earth
that missed my paws.

How strange is my presence
in a space and place losing reverence?

I have arrived,
bear of the mountain.
Every year, this mountain
gets smaller.
Where will I live if they destroy my zoo
for the money, leaving
the earth stripped of its own cloth
that humanity put an unconscious price to?

Where Do I Come From?

I materialize from the dust of the earth.
I appear like sand on beaches.
I pop up from the roots of a great tree.
I walk on earth elevated by godly roots
that rise from the joint of the earth to bone.
I emerge from Mother's Earth heart.
I am moving towards a lineage that has no ending or /
beginning.
I burst out of love and pain.
I became accessible by many grandparents.
I was born out of strong and fragile bones, but I'm always /
at work.
I come from the light, and I am a drop and splash of that
great circle.
I show up like a double rainbow,
and here I am reconnecting with my colors.

I happen to be from the same womb the universe was born in.
I appear after the marriage of heaven and earth.
I come from a jungle that I call my family.
I am a reflection of every living being around me.

Life is covered by God's hand.
Energy has no limited form.
Colors rave and reggae loves.
A weapon is love and defense is peace.

Everyone is a shaman,
and God is the patient we are studying.
Food is a good deed,
and our digestion is the expansion of our deeds.

We kiss God on the forehead,
and God kisses us back with one divine heart.
We are all kites tied to one massive hand.
There is no leader or followers,
just waves crashing into their own existence.
We are all masterpieces walking
without the need for plastic surgeons.
Kindness sweeps away the foolish ways
and opens the portals of a divine mess.

I come from a place where
we bow down to the light in each one.
Children are adorned in patience and love,
rising like lava without exploding.
The stars kiss the moon,
and we kiss the sky goodnight.
We thank the tree for shelter.
We bathe in wet soil to recycle our energies.
Everybody hugs walking hands.

The devil is kissed and given a chance to change.
Evil is muted and negativity is drugged.
The meaning of sorry and the action of love
is recited like program news.
We see the light in everything.
Breaking bread is religious.
Smiling is mandatory.

Hanging a picture of a deceased person
is like hanging a master degree.
Silence is practice and there, we recharge.
We are all exported from

a rainbow soup
that God keeps dripping
and creation continuously keeps seeking.
It is in our best interest to garden each other's soul with love.
and being cheap means disregarding a fallen soul.

Where I come from, we all wear the crown of consideration,
even when the rest of the world doesn't care.
Where I come from, emotional expression is holy
and speaking from the spiral of love is
an essential fragrance.

Her Darkness

When we protect her,
we protect ourselves.

If her darkness is destroyed,
we will never see the light again.

Shield the earth
from heartbreakers
that skipped class when
God was teaching us about love.

Protect her with your heart—
the shield no other men can form for you,
the weapon that rides on the most
emotional part of your design.

Greed is eating her up
like she's worth waste.
They hurt themselves with the same arrow
they launch into the field of her openness.

Let's stand up now
and walk together like
the sky and the earth holding hands.

Let's protect each other
to keep this rainbow land
glowing as much as possible
because Happiness
resides in the compliment
that bleeds out of every single heart.

Shield the earth
and sacrifice yourself
to protect your true soul,
the earth that has given
birth to you once,
bringing you to the light
out the darkness of her womb.

Lunch Break

My roots are growing
and my leaves are spreading.
I'm feeling the heat from Pele.
Pele is the lava I feel under my feet
and the cool breeze I needed from father sky.

Today, I think I know were I'll be...
Life is mysterious,
and thinking too much
leads me to skipping the present.

Standing strong helps me
from not getting lost,
so I'll burn while letting the heat
fire up my stance on this earth.

Mothers

All great mother,
mother battling and dancing on the earth,
you are like the wind that passes by my face.
You are that one rare star in the sky
hidden and watching over blinking stars.
You are the comfort and silence in the night.
You relax me like swirling smoke from incense.
You are as warm as cloth and strong like needles.
Your heart is massive and sometimes unappreciated.
You always forgive; your face hold no grudges.
You are pure love and energy.
You light up like the rocks in the parks.

Labor is daily, and every day, you feel like you're giving birth.
The struggle makes you stronger, and your seeds analyze /
your artwork.

What would this earth be
if we don't protect
and love our mothers?

I Had to Just Grab Your Attention

There's a rhythm
in the air
that makes me fly,
hop, and climb
the mountains' tallest trees—
and from that height,
I jump free without thinking,
flying along a love's open space,
the love I consume,
and sprinkling new feathers with courage.

Nothing is for me to keep
because we all need
to fall in love all over again
with the necessity of our being
and become a divine tribe.

I flap my wings
and release a sensation that we all need.
And I can't keep
what was meant to be broken into pieces.
Like the stream,
the earth divides many parts of me.
Like the ocean, I'm always running.
I'm not sure how to swim,
yet I still get to where I have to be.

I open my heart
to the beat,
hugging every concave being

and learning to trust
sounds that feel like raindrops.
I rub my veins on leaves
with the curiosity of a poet
relearning how to speak.

I run outside of me
to connect with the greater me,
moving to the rhythm
the rain makes
when it touches the earth
that I can't keep.

I am a tune of that great song.
The universe has made a new
instrument out of me,
and now I can make the earth and sky
pause and listen to me.

The Overlooked Prescription

The muse of my peace,
I am the puffer fish hooking itself onto wisdom.
Away from rush hour,
I find the platform of heaven in the woods.

Everyone wants a taste,
But they don't know how to give back.
Capitalism is a lottery game—
Rescue yourself from the sinking holes of expectations.

I hear a butterfly sing to cocoons.
I see bees dancing tango with orchid sunflowers.
I fall in love with life
And thank God for the palette of my creation.

God is the earth's pacifier,
And we are babysitters of a different
part of her body when we play the part
And contribute to her preservation.

A playground
Where good and evil
Find their identity,
I find comfort and peace.

Love knows
The earth's stretch marks
And consults her tears when
No one dares to get close to the consultation
room to hear her complain.

I visit the temple of green dreams
Once in a blue moon to discover
The Enlightenment of My Curiosity
fuelled by the spirit of the earth.

— Remembering and Consulting The Ancestors —

Reclaiming My Power

Here we are in the present
remembering our ancestors
through artifacts
left behind so we pick them like toys
and redesign the story of our clans.

Playing drums, we dance merengue,
erasing the chase of heaviness.
We used to be composed slaves.
Now we are a liberated album
that no one can place a price on.

We walk like caciques
and hold our meditation pose like yucca roots.
We no longer accept human abuse
We are the Indians of this time
walking in strange clothes.

Natives to great beings,
natives of simplicity,
natives with humility,
natives because of the past,
and strangers in modernization.

Our spirit is sown
in spiritual wealth.
We are beginning
to reclaim this
from our ancestral lineages.

Reborn Tribal Member

We are all beautiful,
and it doesn't matter
where we live:
Distance doesn't separate beauty.
Distance gives beauty space to become more beautiful.

Let's maintain being at peace
with our neighboring trees.
The trees are keepers of our history.
Who will share the stories of our lives
if keep we sawing down the rings
that archive our growth span?

Let's protect
our true home,
our true shelter,
the nest our tummies fell in love with at first site.

Let's look inside ourselves
and reconnect with the good
in our beings.
Let's put aside the sorrows
that carry our bodies.

There's medicine
in our souls.
Everywhere we go, there is medicine.
There isn't one place that's perfect—
God is, not a nearby pharmacy.

Sorrows pollute the soul with tyranny.
Let's branch like our neighboring trees,
feel our culture deeply within,
and heal our pain,
awakening our true art.

Ask yourself:
What is your medicine?
When did you stop sharing it?
Who's your animal guide?
Why did you stop consulting the great one?
Who is your teacher?
Why did the lessons stop coming?

Look inside your history,
look inside the trees.

Where did you leave your heart behind?
Where did it all go wrong?
Have you lost human joy?

Look in your history
to find your present glow—
a glow you never lost,
a glow you forgot you always had within you.

Look in to the present
and respect the glow of others
that have risen out of their history.

Promise of the Elders

I work like a dog during the day
to rest like a cat in the night.

I work like a garden
to see baby snails become adults.

I work like a lighthouse
to share material triumphs with you.

I work until the pigment of my skin fades
to be the masterpieces I leave for you to study.

I used to race with time.
Now I let time race alone.
I have found time to share all my love with you,
even when dreams and bills invaded
my true priority, my family.

I'll be the petroglyphs
in a lesson I pass to you
so you never feel alone.

My son, I'm the light that'll continue
to shine because you are the outlet
that the divine won't separate me from,
even when I pass.

Offering of Thankfulness

Coffee and sweets!
I have just lit
another candle for the spirit
of my tribe.

The sound of my maraca!
Hear my offering;
I am a grateful being.

I don't erase the struggle of my people
to remind me that we migrate like birds
and eat like a pack of wolves.
Everyone gets a piece of the loaf.

My body is a carnival.
In my blood, there's a lineage
of migrators with humble dreams.

Coffee and sweets!
I'm proof that butterflies don't die;
They just expand
into the cocoon of the next generation's dues.

I let the divine fan
the flames that my ancestors
have been preserving,
so I stand like the volcano
that's willing to explode spiritually
at any peak he's placed on.

Divine Voice

My son don't waste no time.
He thinks so much
that even his good thoughts have bad deeds.

Invest time in action.
Use your artistic machete
to open the way, not enclose yourself.

Get dressed to get dirty at work
and undress love
while you clean yourself up.

Swallow with pleasure
those things a clean heart can only desire.
But don't eat what the hand
wants when they are dirty and undeceived.

God has become my trustworthy cane
and silence has become my best friend.

See how animals walk on land.
They will teach you how to walk
in new ways.

My son, beyond your eyes
and conscience I stay.
Go there, and I'll wait
for you waiting for me
within you.

Coffee Time

While having coffee with my ancestors,
don't forget who your investor is.
You better be living your best life.
To become the Professor,
God loves to return to class and hear you speak.
Always remember to send the Diviner love letters
and remember all your mentors
like you never forget your favorite sweater
Let your discipline be the compressor.
that keeps us here with you.

Everyone wants me to believe that you're polyester,
but I love staring at you like you an antique poster.
I catch myself strolling in the light of your art center.
My neighbor stares at me and wonders whose jester I mimic.
Doctors would say I'm hallucinating and test me with /
psychotic medicine
because I'm hearing voices.

God, tame my desire to be a gangster.
I became the warrior this semester.
I wanted to see the elders change my diaper daily.
As I paint in colors, I think I'm grown
till God reminds me
I'll always be a dependent baby.
Even if I left my mother's home,
I am continuously mentored by flowers
in gardens learning to survive
through the art of remembering
and consulting my ancestors.

Bodyguard

The great one from my past has spoken...

We are the slime behind snails.
We are the wind behind ravens.
We are the sun behind the moons.
We are the change behind nature.
We are the mountains behind the valleys.

The banknotes behind a bank.
The loyal behind the loyal seeker.
Burnt rubber markings behind young drivers.
The poems behind Sufis.
The meditations behind a disciple.
The rituals behind wise men.
The trails of countless Buddhas.
The trees nailed to Jesus.

We are the bees behind a panel.
We are the machines behind the light.

The eyes behind the lens.
The passion behind a forgotten chef.
The romance between the brush and its painter.
The tears of a broken man.
The scars unfolding right along the hip of her breast.
The echo of every hand-made instrument.
The anxiety of every new parent.
The journey behind the trails.
The soul behind the flesh.
The garden of life behind working hands.

The roar of a rooster behind the sun
All the tentacles behind an insect's head.
The grains and rings behind wooden bats.
The veins on your forehead.
The silencer of gossip.
The messenger of protection.
The invisible behind your visibility.
The orchestra that carries you with love and struggle.
The chauffeur of a car that trusts its mechanic.
An entire collection of flowers staring at the sun for hours.
Permanent tattoos that don't sting but stick.

We are your natural bodyguards,
and if you remember us daily,
we are the people you see daily.
Rise and fall under roots
that no one can spray pesticide on or burn.
We are your ancestors
and you are the life
that we promise the divine we will watch over.

Advice from My Ancestors

With one hand, I want you to work.
With the other hand, I want you to save.
With one leg, rest for a while
and with the other leg, I want to work really hard.

Save the money of your sweat
so when you can't stand up like before,
you don't suffer like you suffer standing all day.

My child, I'm by your side,
and god is the sleeping bag
that covers the spirit of our bodies.

Use one side of your mind for the day
and use the other side of your mind for your night.
To use your presence fully before going to bed,
use our old ways to survive
and mix them with the modern ones to coexist
without losing the rhythm of your essence.

In this game, we play existence.
Love with your whole heart
and with the part of your heart that you never thought
needed a brush to express.

Call on your grandfathers and grandmothers.
They have a lot of tips specially saved for you
if you log into their realm
and don't sign out of God's ways.

Words of Higher Beings

Let people do what they like to do
so you can focus on what you have to do.
Open your hands and heart like and orchid.
Take your time on this landscape;
It is neither a sprint nor a marathon.
Grow like a cactus and spread like mint.
Be flexible like bamboo.
Under God's design, I function.
I'm the puppet tied to strings that dance
according to god chant.
Don't live on express mode.
Rather, hop on a local ride
and admire everything.
You spin your eyes on.
No one is going to be able
to work the land like you do.
You know best.

Your gift is your gift.
Even though we are wrapped under the same bow,
become the master of borrowed dreams
that truly belong to no one.
Be an example to the seed that sprouts
to be in your place one day.
The ancestors see me with the eyes of God.
Don't forget: wisdom is not far
from the wink of your eyes.

— TEACHERS OF NATURE —

The Mountain of Wisdom

Inside every mountain, there is a spirit taking care of me.
Below each mountain, there is a spirit that wants to collapse
my inner mountain.

Whisper at the peak.
Build your house using pieces of each mountain.
But you don't want to build a house on every mountain.
Whisper to the valley because
you will die without seeing the landscape of your sweat.
It is healthier to want less and act more.

Walking less would save you some time.
You'll be able to see more from the perspective of your still-
ness.

Don't go to the sea to catch all the fish.
Stay close to the river near your home.
The biggest fish will come from the sea of your faith.

Remember that patience killed ambition's hunger,
even when ambition is choking patience.

Listen to the voice behind the body, God's gift you.
Don't hide from the truth your heart has already witnessed.

Close your eyes.
Breathing invites meditation,
and when breathing out,
see the truth peeling fruits.

I am a father
and a human.
I am a mountain.
I am God's creations
simplifying my formation.

Be the nation that walks on fresh grass.
Be the station that donates seeds of love.
Solitude is key for the peeling of the soul.
Cremate all thoughts that don't let the soul burn happy.
Coexist like patches on a dalmatian.

Donate your present to the sketches that God paints daily.
Stay out of the Department of Nature Detention.
Carry no one's frustration.
Ask the earth and the sky for my hydration.
Be someone's sensation.

To concentrate on the Earth train station, burn all space /
stations.
Let flowers and hidden gardens be your temptation.
Request no translation; instead, be your own life /
transformation.
Take a trance-state meditational vacation.
Become the vibration that trips an excavation.

Let no one alter the royalty of your creation.
Amputate the fungus that doesn't let your heart
feel divine orgasmic liberation.
Cancel all negative frequencies arising from
anyone who is causing inner peace segregation.

Life is more of a celebration than a demonstration.
Decorate your life with the secrets God whispers
through the mouth of trees seeking to converse about
ecological spirituality.

Everyone wants a reservation
to go to heaven, but they have taken the wrong medication.
Be the raven that stands out
in this beautiful generation with so much information.

Stay away from spiritual discrimination.
Judging no one is your obligation.
Let's rise to become a green civilization!
Now, use your damn imagination.

Life is my elevation.
God is my divination
The Earth, my education.
And my spiritual journey has been a pollination.

My fascination is the wood trail.
My curiosity is self-fermentation.
Healing is my fragmentation
as the Earth becomes my power station.

When We Got United

The hurricane has no feelings.
Vengefulness takes everything in the middle
without thinking who lives.
In the center of that environment,
revenge has no heart.

I don't know who sent it...
Maybe it was a person without a heart.
Sorry that I speak of your massacre
as if I don't have a heart.
But after taking many lives
from my heart and my eyes,
I feel empty yet filled with questions
of love and destruction.

Slaughter is a fire in the breeze
eating all the trees we live by.
The storm has no address
or eye-for-eye coming for our homes.
Prepare to move
or hide
into the next neighborhood.

Violence is something alive
promoted by every gossip in the news.
Extinction has no emotions.
He does not cry or hug.
His embrace is a downfall
and her drop of tears
that suffocates my home.

Avengement has no opinion.
Hatred is at war with us.
He comes for his mission
and on our side of the fight
has nothing we can hold on to
as we receive
the blows of the hurricane.

What can we do
when nature spanks us?
Learn to be a community
and hang on to
each other,
spelling out:
ayni, anyi[1].

1. The Quechua word for this mutuality is "ayni", meaning "today for you, tomorrow for me," suggesting that giving comes before receiving. "Ayni" is the only commandment of the Incan religion that the Andeans know and keep until this day. Ayni is the thread that holds the fabric of Andean existence together. Ayni involves all the relationships that exist among the Andean people as well as their relationship with Mother Earth, Pachamama.

Walking like a Snail

Stop running away from your home—
the home that has always been in you,
that no one can vacate you from: your soul.
You are your own shelter.
Stop searching for walls!

You must take your time with life
to move at the pace
that the sweat of your trails desires.

The unnatural would runs you over,
crushes you in rush hours,
and tosses your organs in express lanes.

Life is a circle.
Look at the trail on my shell,
and you'll see the reflection
of a pattern folding and unfolding

like all forms of life
take the same steps of yesterday
to be woken up by today,
greeted by God's breath,
the chants of sparrows
and rooftop crows.

Your body is your home.
Let god be the locksmith of your door.
You must know every wall
that forms your walk.

If life becomes a thing of night,
you must always become the light.
Let no one unplug your shine.
Let your faith be the umbilical chord
that no one can cut you from.

Learn and relearn to take your time.
Give no one access to hold
the control of your paces.
Be the channel
the divine loves watching
and the series that Mother Earth is hooked on.

Your body is your home.
Greet everyone with it
with the same love.
But don't let everyone into the sanctuary.
You must upkeep
throughout the day and night.

Visions of an Old Friend

Pretty tall giraffe.
Yes, you are.

Tallest of them all.
Yes, you are.

Your presence
I didn't see in me before—
The kids did,
but I ignored your call.
I apologize.

My ignorance grew because
elementary kids had the longest smile
and cracked jokes on me.

Yet I didn't know
that the jokes were hidden messages.
I didn't catch on.

You faded away from my life
as my denial got lost in sports,
and I pulled away from your medicine.

Today, as you step on my back
and my eyes are closed,
I breathe in this new heaviness
of old energy reviving me
as I walk on Mother Earth Runway.

I know if I let you go this time,
it's because you must return to your tribe of spots
because now I am ready to paint mine.

You're pretty tall giraffe.
Yes, you are.

The Hurricane

Get inside that hurricane
so the yesterday of you dies today
like many of us leave,
driving fast lanes.

Get inside that hurricane!
Let it be your designer,
preparing you for a better today
and undressing you from any migraine.

Get inside that hurricane!
Let it take you through a bird's brain
till you learn to see the light
after your transformation.

Get inside that hurricane!
'Cause it's time to change.
Don't you want to feel like a Great Dane?

I am the hurricane—
the medicine of destruction
reflecting light from darkness
with what of you remains.

The Flautist

Sitting in the back of the house
with incense burning
and the hunger of my pencil
consuming paper,
I listen to the breeze.

Fainting, I catch myself in a state,
desiring to write
a poem to the breeze...

Breeze, you sing
to all the leaves and make them lean like plantains.
Breeze, the crickets use you as their alarm.
Now the night sings
a song from the sounds of the fields.
Breeze, you rock back and forth
the youth in every being—
It doesn't matter
how young or old the shell of their egg is.
Yolk is yolk wherever it lives.

Breeze, you tell me in silence
that the best way to love the moment
is by enjoying everything
that is present
in front of me and not far away.
Because sometimes, it's better to feel than to see.
Because the breeze that went to the other side
never returns back.
So just admire
everything that is of a quick second.

Breeze you are the flautist of the land.
I have been hearing you
sitting in the back of the house
and giving the land your lungs
for the peace you have
gained in your heart.

The Bee of Freedom

Dancing with honey,
bees obey their queen.
A happy society
arises when
work is seen as a divine opportunity.

Society is no different
than a panel of bees
walking and flying.
We meet our needs.

Find me a job, queen of the earth,
and I'll bring you what feeds your soul.
Spreading honey all over nature,
love finds it ways in every rose.

Honey bonds people and nature.
Bees are the best council
of sweetness and bitterness.
Protecting was sacred,
the work remains a space for devotion.

Mess with my peace,
and you'll see thorns grow out of wax.
Honor your sweat
and treat other nicely
as you transform
while the buzzing calms down
and enlightenment
sets you free.

Rooted, Grounded, Solid

Tree o tree,
help ground me
so when I move on this earth,
my movements are grounded.
Rooted within this earth, **I am**.

Let the actions of my body be
as strong as your trunk:
Rooted, grounded, solid.

Let my arms extend and curve like your branches:
Rooted, grounded, solid.

Let my hair grow and fall like your leaves:
Rooted, grounded, solid.

Let my skin take on seasonal vitamins as every cycle
brings a new glow:
Rooted, grounded, solid.

Let my awareness rise from the bottom of the earth
to the tip of your branches:
Rooted, grounded, solid.

Tranquil, I would extend
because behind every standing tree, there's a party happening:
trees spinning and tap dancing
that only special eyes can see.

Grounded in this middle world,
your roots extend to the lower world
downward to the source of life,
and the hands of your branches slam-dunk into the /
upper world.
The beauty of life, expanding.
Wow. I just finished seeing it all,
and I am part of this expansion!

On and In, In and On

On that tree
and in that flower,
in that crow
and in that human,
we are all connected
like different tattoos
made with the same ink
and placed on top of each other
like layers of paper,
layers of tree rings,
layer of forms,
forming one ultimate
me in you,
you in me,
us in us,
all in one,
one in all
formed.

All beauty that resists
has to join.
All beauty that recognizes
sees with the eyes of the Great Spirit
with no self, no division, no ego, no preference
to claim mine.

— Anthony Guzman —

Nature Is My Teacher

O great guidance counselor of nature,
I am here in your presence
to learn from your ways
so I can understand myself
through your help
in a walking dream
where the moon records
and the sun saves
the effort of my growth.

O great disciple of the earth,
I am here knocking on the branch
of your door to be risen by the elevator of your wisdom
onto a floor of learning and forming
a new relationship with you
as we sit in this class called The Universe.

Leaping in a flight of growth,
God grades me by my presence
upon this earth.

O great mentor of oneness,
we are here to become one and merge,
exchanging body-forms in visions
and play out the cure in real life-form.

As crows sew wings on my back
and I ride on a giraffe hump
running in circles with squirrels,
I drag my soul through the land like a snail,

buttoning my actions with love
and reminding myself that even if I fall,
there's another branch I can leap on
'cause life is a forest that falls and rises,
re-nurturing all generations that pass.

My Initiation

Understood by animals.
I went to the woods
invited by an ally crow
'cause nobody understood me in society.
During a breaking point,
I was looking for answers
to questions that people's curiosity didn't crave.

In the woods,
my body melted
on top of a rock while meditating.
I became a shining rock
while the sun pierced my heart with light,
giving me a new form of eyesight.

In the woods,
I became one with all the spirits around me
both good and bad.
From the bad one, I learned that unexpected things
happen when you drop your spiritual guard.
From the good, I learned how to live life
as an adventure and God's final direction.

Confused and alone,
I found friends and companionship
with worms that came out the earth
and squirrels that chanted morning songs.

Parks became my refugee
as I played a game
called questions of the heart
in a hidden society
that gave birth to a new mystic.

I found a special barn behind brick buildings,
breaking loose from the street life and drugs
and touring a spark of wisdom,
a never-ending high of tranquility
in the woods that gave me an answer.

Loyalty in Nature

Loyal is a crow
to his pact
like winter to snow.

Loyal is a snail
to his shell
like a tree is to native ground.

Loyal is a squirrel
to is tree
like penguins migrate across the mine of soft ice.

Loyal is a snake
to his trail
like toilet seats to bellyaches.

Loyal is a giraffe
to his beauty mark
like a splash of waves are to a rock.

Loyal is the sun
to the morning
like pearls attached to its shells.

Loyal is the moon
to the night
like parks full of raccoons.

Loyal is the boat
to his water waves
like the bay tied its houseboat.

Loyalty is the ocean
touching the sand
on the same point
at the same time.

Kick out the Rainbow

Bless these beads,
black on black.
The rainbow
kicks you out of the pact
because you sang the truth.

I wear the truth around my body
to represent my connection with you
because I dislike painting lies in saturated colors.

Crow, you fly up above
while I fly from below.
I admire your moves.
Can I borrow a flight with you?

You seem to find your way up above,
so must I find my way from below.
I hear your song everywhere I go.

Let's turn into bread dough.
Let our bodies and spirits merge.
In this vision, we must flow.

You'll fly, I'll fly.
You'll make noise, I'll make noise.
You'll rest and I'll rest.

You'll build and I'll build.
You'll mate and I'll mate.
You'll land and I'll land.

You move in your pact,
and God will send me mine
while I wear these beads,
representing the sound of truth.

Dear Crow

The feathers that hang off my ears speak to me
while the voice within the feather
harps along strands of our body and spirit.

It is a complete musical piece of you and me,
a presence
that transforms.

Our eyes close,
inviting the cakes of our dough
to mold
wings from by back
so I can fly as far as you can,
making my lips vocalize what I couldn't say before,
helping me feel the blueprint of my feet,
and borrowing the hunt of your catch.

I dance spiritually amongst the trees
that watch me express my spiritual needs.

Crucified Snake

O good snake,
don't let the bad snakes
spoil every good snake's day.

Who's bad is bad;
who's good is good.
Bad and good don't mix.

Even though they are
two different snake trails
in the same landscape,
a good snake leaves a trail
marked by good deeds
and a bad snake leaves a trail
marked with bad deeds.
Every trail returns to its origin.

Ask yourself,
which snake are you going to be:
the good snake fighting
to maintain its pieces
or the bad snake consuming
the serenity in others
to convert them into "snakes"
that Christianity condemns them to be?

Autumn

Oh breeze,
connected to heaven,
moving me with the earth,
passing my body—

The same breeze
I felt pass in the past
that unites us to warm our cold body
with hugs.

Oh breeze,
invisibly passing through me,
telling me that the times
changes from warm to cold
like an affectionate woman
can freeze in time
if she's not covered by a rose
that understand her thorns.

Oh breeze
that shakes the fabric of my body,
drying my lips and inspiring my being
to seek survival in nature's changes.

Oh breeze,
I was missing you during summertime.
Today I feel you again,
and my body trembles
like the muffler of an old car.

There is a breeze that makes me sick and heals me,
knocking the mucus out of my head,
cleaning my brain and opening my nose.

As the breeze grabs the orange leaves of autumn
from old trees that are tired of carrying dead leaves,
there is a breeze that cleanses our body
like the river cleans algae from rocks on the shore.

There is a breeze that reminds me:
Winter misses the sun,
and we weren't made to love and live alone.

Advice from a Snail

A snail crossed my path,
leaving a message written on its slime:
Gentlemen, take care of your spirit
like I take care of my shell.
The only thing you have
is the most precious armor of your spirit a body.

It fights to maintain peace
inside the time that your time gives you
so you learn that peace is
produced by the speed of your own movement
and the steps that you alone understand.

Young men paint the earth with your trail
the same way I paved the way
as I reached far places on this earth
without letting my true self be misguided or destroyed
by city rush hours or express train rides amongst anxious men.

Evolving men,
rub with your soles
every pebble of the earth.
Feel the fullness of experience
one pebble at a time.
At your own pace, touch everything
that feeds the peace of your being
in a landscape
of beings rushing time,
expiring before being enlightened,
living life as a short series,
and not fulfilling
all the pages of their entire book.

A Tree in Rage

Just because you think I don't have hands,
        I can't touch.
Just because you think I don't have eyes,
        I can't see.
Just because you think I don't have feet,
        I can't walk.
Just because you think I don't bleed,
        I don't live.
Just because you think I don't have a mouth,
        I can't eat.
Just because you don't witness any of these things
      on me doesn't mean
        they don't exist.

Maybe I do have the same body parts
that you do, my human relative.
You must see me with the eyes of a child.
Give me the chance to show you
what I am capable of sharing with you.
I'm of the many trees in our environment
that yearns to be touched,
heard and fed, and to live
the same way you live—
to touch, eat, walk, and see!

Give me a chance
when you are ready to drop
your lack of perception
because I'm that part of nature
that gets ignored
by humans that have forgotten
to admire the wonder that stands behind stillness.

A Date with the Moon

O dear moonlight,
you are my knight,
you are my light,
you are my date in the night,
guiding me to the direction
where my lips shift into a smile.

I am another star
in the expanse of your light bulb.
I am a sparkle the resonates with those
who greet you in the nighttime.
I am the star you always spin back into your bobbing.

The table we sit on
is half sky and half earth.
We don't sit alone:
The trees watch us
as we make their dead bark shed in joy.

The distance the universe creates
only keeps us connected.
You look at me with my eyes
and I look at you with your eyes.
Our hearts belong to neither one,
just to the spark of this park that has witnessed
all of this.

On My Own Lane

When I take my time on this earth
like a snail, sloth, and turtle,
I enjoy life,
seeking no destiny
at the speed of my true nature.

But when I run around like
a cheetah, ostrich, and dinosaur,
I miss the important
points of my life.

Once again losing myself within the rush,
a snail, a sloth, and turtle
invades my plane with truth,
telling me to get back up,
be patient
and be one with the speed of my own body.

Just don't you give in
to the rush
that wants to drive
your true nature crazy
into lanes
that don't even recognize
the struggle of your footprints.

Everybody runs
on a different engine type.
Some people ride on a toxic road
while other engines know
how to ride along the curve of an icy road.

Can you move at
the nature of your own divinity?
Challenge your own need to be fidgety,
borrowing god meditative pose.

Everybody has a special playbook.
Every soul has a different route
as we all try to score the touchdown
of self-gratitude,
a spiritual satisfaction.

I can walk in your shoes,
but you can't tie them for me.
I must seek the fruit
that empowers
the bitter part of an aching body.

I don't want to be rushed
by survival.
I want to be taken for a walk
by the hands of the great shaman.

— THE BEGINNING OF HEALING —

Mother Earth,
how do you recuperate
after natural disasters?

The moon and the sun
pulley me up.
My roots become my stitches.
During spring I am bandaged,
and in summer, my wounds are dry.
And I rise.

God kisses my forehead.
The storm chants.
The rain massages my body.
And I rise.

My ants march under a new anthem, and I revive.
Crickets play maracas, and I dance.
My rock resists every hit.
And if I crack, I cement my way back.
And yet again, I rise.

Ecologists educate me on myself, and I'm stunned.
I trust that even I, the earth, needs to change.
Being stagnant is false.
So I again rise.

Because if I can bench-press the city,
you unfairly build over my back.
I believe you, my son,
can also heal from the trauma
that weighs you down.

My branches fall
so new hands can grow.

Overworking the soul leaves the body with no juice to rejoice /
in the world.
So learn to hammock yourself into the earth and rest in /
God's design.
If your hair falls like autumn sings
and white hair breaks into your party unexpected,
you can also intervene in the habits that break you down.

Water the dim no one believes can harness fresh water.
Learn from the ways miracles are sketched.
Even nature gets inspired by the brush
that changes everyone's situation.

Kindness and Compassion

Trust that God speaks within you.

Create a nest for kindness.
Become the bamboo that goes where water crawls.

Cover your body with the fleece it loves.
Transport your ache
from earth that no longer holds it growth.

Love the reflection of yourself first
and share what you discover
without losing your ticket.

The body is the stroller
of the soul.
Make sure you weigh like a feather
while living your best adventure.

Life is not a rock that
you have move out the way;
it's one you must greet
to not get lost around the experience.

Every new day,
hand yourself the power
to be kind and compassionate.
Merge both within
and loosely with all intent
that inspires the routine release.

Let the body
become a kindness spoon,
releasing action of compassion
so everyone can reincarnate into buds
that trust the sun.

I'm going to pamper all of me
and share with the world a percentage of this.

Let it rain emotion
from ever being
I am already a part of.

Compassion sits and listens to relatives
that need a therapist in each one.

No one can strip me from
the food, the mind, and the gut's needs.
Perseverance and confidence are key.

Humanity is God's gift,
and I experience romanticism with
the wisdom nature conveys to me.

Can't you see
that smiles unfold the premature flower in you
and kindness makes a homeless man
believe in food again?

I have marked souls on my path
by my way of being,
tattooing their hearts
with the love God hands me.

I am a shamanic recipe,
a Taoist surrounded by a temple of metal and glass,
a Buddhist that wears the rainbow,
a mystic borrowing love from every belief.

Treat yourself like the baby of God
and don't mistreat your soft aging skin.

Kindness empties the gun
and compassion
regrets the trigger pulled.

Pamper the body,
powder the soul,
and Wipe the mind with vibrant colors.

Life should be a yoga session,
not a weight-lifting class.
Exercise the dance with the soul and its body.

I am stepping into a fauvist lifestyle,
a surreal reality that recycles experience,
a fantasy that I can process.

So let your problems be your therapist
and the solution be God's recipe.

Kindness and compassion
are the teachers that await
for you to attend the class
of personal experience.

How Does Praying Help Us Heal?

An overloaded tree
asks for help
and an overly styled mannequin
asks for relief.

The lungs liberate!
Now the mind
has new bed sheets.

The temple that stores all my words,
the libraries that harness all my breath,
my request hung in an old closet...

I tell you the secret humans can't keep,
the poems no one hears,
the tears and smiles you keep.

How do I detach?
What can't I bench-press?
What can't I bask underneath?

A congested soul
never experiences the magic of prayer.
God softens the soul.
Interchange
what you can't do alone.

Rain amulets and charms
of prayers on the dispiriting within
now applaud the new that steps in.

In the cave of the divine
are the echoes missing your speech.
Preach your true need
and disqualify your unnecessary wants.

Call on the winds
that spread
the ink you hold within.

If love meets you inside,
you must travel with the ticket
God implanted you with.

A private session,
a reunion,
a sit-in
with I and I.

Unclogging my speech
makes me ask
for the simple things
I can actually see.

A conversation with an imaginary friend
everybody claims behind walls,
I claim within me.

Prayers erase a centimeter of my wounds,
and I must erase the next inch.

Expressing my true needs,
I obtain and maintain,
preserving the reality God helped me upkeep.

Can you introduce to the divine
an incomplete song
and trust that writing together
is better than writing alone?

Prayers are heard by ears.
Always open
and warm hearts.
Don't give up on the one
that has already read
the journal you write in.

There is a new generation
that we must prune and mentor.
With love, share songs that uplift
the one shedding diapers and pacifiers.

Prayers are a power song
that make you walk in a new rhythm,
relating in different ways.

Grasp the simplicity
chaos has stolen you from,
praying for the return of a new reality:
Buddha and Jesus married.

I am more
resilient and confident,
lighter and happier,
freer and more curious
when I exchange prayers
for nothing in return.

I walk behind the body
that listens to my prayer
like a baby duck,
baby chick,
an infant learning how to walk.

A special call,
private message
from and to,
to and from...
The contact
I have no reason to block:

Prayer empties
the tsunami's waves
I carry inside me.
It can be anything
that stops me from surfing
the purpose I give
and the life given to me.

I have fallen on the pillow
that knows my mold best.
I'm happy to cry.

I'm the man
that sprouts from the valley of wildflowers,
and every season, hears
the change of my growth.

Today hears my morning prayer
and the thank you note

I leave kissed on an ancient tree
and new clouds.

The more you love me,
the better you know me.
Love knows the better me
and inspires me
to look forward to meeting
the future me.

I carry no weapon
or narcotics
to lift me or protect me.

Kindness and compassion
defrost the fears that blind the spiritless.
I am the spirit shining on the earth
that glows out of its own nature.

I pray for commuters
who haven't lost faith
and the new one they found.

Under the same sunlight
that covers all of us
with the same eyes,
prayers pollinate
and revive a tribe of bees.
Can you trust where love hides?
In your honeycomb,
and brush me with the same raw honey
God serves all.

You can lose faith,
change beliefs,
change colors,
plug in and plug out...

But never stop
checking in with the God
who will raise you back up
during all your falls and rises.

To the one who takes a break
to listen to your prayers
and replies with
the expression
of the peace and happiness
that belongs to you.

How Does Affirmation Help Me Heal?

Tell yourself what negativity doesn't want you to know.
Affirmation is a map that guides me once again.
Buttons that make me look sharp.

Affirmation is the savior of my head,
God's personal secret for me.
These couture words of encouragement
were designed specifically for me.

An alarm clock, a reminder, a firework
spelling out the progression of my soul—
a personal song or poem that only I know.

At my lowest, I'm risen by a boost,
the inspiration of my high,
the commandments of my dress forms.

The gauze of my wounds,
The Silencer of Negative Talk,
recipes extracted from forgotten alphabets.

Whispers of ancestral aid,
miracles giving birth to patients' liberation.

Confirmation of the iron motif in my mind,
fossils I discovered during my meditation trips.

The gold I forgot to see within,
the trophy I must give myself daily,
a toss with fragmentation.

Wounds are beauty marks,
and every living being is a warrior of some kind.
Somehow, keep your head
within the grass above the rain.

I take a ride on a butterflied snake,
the dragon in me roaring
and casting fire and ice on my peace.

I have learned to baby-sit the affirmations.
God has given them to me until the time comes
to return them to the universes where they came from.

How Do the Arts Help Us Heal?

O great spirit, o great teachers of nature,
o great ancestors, o great elements,
teach me..

We are all creators.
pushing out the invisible
from orgasmic inspiration.

The body is an art studio,
hiding masterpieces.
Share the secret you and the brush share.

Share what the heart stores
and your stomach can't digest.
What prefers to live outside your mouth?
Words that inspire the soul.

Adorn the body that slowly falls
with pearls and beads
that tease the light within.

Express the essence of your thought
on simple paper
and mediums that can digest your thoughts.

Be possessed by the spirit of art.
Mediums know what recipe
your tongue craves.

Lift what hides
in the water hole.

The depths of your soul reflects
the dome God sleeps in.

What sense does it make
to leave a brush untouched?
A young hand free from wrinkles.

My brain is a sketch book,
my heart is a journal,
and art is the final piece.

I built the nest
that carries all my weight
on the branch I trust.

The canvas carries all my stitches.
The easel awaits my arrival.
I make anxiety and peace share love.

I give to life first
what is in me,
introducing you to my world.

I understand myself
through the reflection of art,
hammocked and hypnotized by instruments
I'll invite to all stages I live in.

Become clay
and trust the invisible hand,
crafting a new you out of the same sand
that your problems are made of.

All my attention is stolen
by a drawing that escapes from the dance of my wrist
onto the dance floor of brand new paper.

God made me an artist,
but you don't have to be one
to express your soul.

Poetry is my medicine,
painting shapes while waiting to be married to words.
I'm the brush that goes through stages.

Art is a hospital
with rooms full of inspiration.
You should play with all the mediums
that give your voice a home.

I repeat again:
I'm possessed by inspiration
and I am enlightened.

Silence loves creativity,
and walls witness
the frustration of every soul
that's been pulled away from what they love.

Art may be a medium you can purchase,
but no one can buy a spiritual experience.

I build myself like a masterpiece.
I'm a never-ending landscape,
a surreal dream, always adding to the canvas.

We are all tattoos with dreams and vision.
Choose the medium.
that waters your fear,
awakening personal satisfaction of self-love.

Art is not a selling experience;
rather, a healing session.

Be the one
who inspires the spirit of art

Become the palette
that God picks from,
turning life into your favorite canvas.

No one knows
the voice
you listen to daily.
Make it a beautiful song.

Art is the prescription.
God left humanity
before the medicine
was called art.

When I awaken...
the museum I always visit,
the poem I always feel,
the colors I keep close to me;

the song I continuously dedicate to myself,
a palace and luminous castle within;

the song they don't play on radio,
the one I alarm
when I awaken.

My first affirmation,
and the tunnel is once again open
with possibilities I never dreamed of.

An expressive purification,
a creative ritual,
words marking every tomb and womb.

I am the hero of my own story.
My power arrives
in the ways I relate to God's creation.

I give the day
the bravery of my heart
and the authenticity of my breath.

My friend, you are the canvas I paint on.
My friend, you are the person I express my poem to.
God is the grace of every day.

Celebrate Your Life Daily

Celebrate the absence of what you bury.
Celebrate the presence of what you know best.
Step into the party
that life prepares for you
and God arranges.

Celebrate the decay,
the songs you make when you stump the earth
with dreams that she helps you nurture.

Celebrate the tired body.
Celebrate the signals bar
you and God transmit on.

Celebrate the smiles that are still alive
and the new one
that sleeps behind the premature one.

Celebrate this canvas
God once again painted for us.
Decide which being you'll be today
and choose the pigments:
Niagara blue, sandal gold, metallic green
that make more light come out of me.
Celebrate the mystery
of how words escape the soul,
pushed out by the intention of who knows.

Celebrate everyone's journey.
Don't skip complimenting all of life.
God continues drawing us when we love each other.

Celebrate the deep breath
You've got to give back to the space around you
and experience what the brain draws.

Celebrate losing control
and gaining trust,
forgiving and remembering
the best part of you that always can and will.

Become the cake
God offers every day.
Let no one blow your candle
with bitter souls.

Romanticize the soul
God married to your mind and flesh
to make your world a better place to live in.

Fuck the news
and the sorry-tales
that give birth to fear and hate.

Can I pop you out the balloon you hide in my son?
Can I pull you out of the table you hide in my daughter?
I design life so you can celebrate yours.

Animal Power

Become the messenger's mailbox.
Trust is a leap of faith.
Find a teacher you can rely on.
Let God whisper in your ears.
Clean your heart with its clothes.
Immerse your wound in the source.
Believe in the spirit of the spirit.

Find your home in the teachers
and let your ache fall into the recycle bin.
Trust the spirit
that nurtures the fragile soul.
Shelter your love
and know your intent.
Trust the spirit of the spirit
that comes with an adoption form,
an exchange no one else has to know about.

Trust the spirit of the spirit
that knows the true needs
in response to your melting request.
Dive into the medical field,
the realm of wisdom,
the spirit world,
the ancestral playground.

Trust the spirit of the spirit.
Observe how animals interact with their surroundings
and plug in the solution
to your field of thought.

Pierce the dragon by its heart.
and tame the painful part.

Trust the spirit of the spirit.
God made us to serve each other.
Please assist me with your cawing techniques.
Support my flight, butterfly.

Trust the spirit of the spirit.
Illuminate the invisible thread
that holds the key to our existence.
Let everyone see oneness.

Trust the spirit of the spirit.
I'm not going to fight the battle for you
but teach you how to fight with
the strength oppressed from within.

Trust the spirit of the spirit.
Don't abandon
the spoon
that feeds every centimeter
you keep rooted within you.

Trust the spirit of the spirit.
Anchor all of yourself
on the medicine wheel
that is aware of the diagnosis
and appetite in you.
Faith is a leap of trust.

Ungratefulness is like betrayal.
Keep everything I taught you with you.
The calling of a teacher and the reunion of its student
is a road trip you must embark on.

God makes no mistakes.
Send each soul its totem for reasons
genetic and DNA tests can't report
Scan your faith under God's wings
and forget to fly until you learn how to walk again.

Trust the spirit of the spirit
that's here to take you out
of the shell you've created
and in the crate society shapes for you.

Healing doesn't believe in calendars or time,
but cycles that complement
when you are trusting the process or not.

Smiling and forgetting,
ritualizing and loving...
Content and thankful soul,
heal according to the check God signed first.

There are a lot of spears and gourds
and many thick skins and glaciers
that are ready to take a hit for you,
but can the words of your heart beat faster?
Screaming out thanking you, God,
and killing the words the ego loves first,
I did this alone.

Can you
trust the spirit of the spirit
that knows you better than you know yourself?
Can you
trust the spirit of the spirit
to heal you
during your cycles
like the earth knows her season?

Reinventing Myself

Changing pages, I'm a calendar
with new phases.
I'm a multicolored mannequin
comfortable with many branded clothes.
Nakedness stores the truth of my creation.
I design myself according to the way the season makes my /
soul feel.

Stop trying to heal what has passed your hand.
Feed and spoon the today
that comes from the trembling horizon.
Be the morphed butterfly and snake
that call out your new name.

It doesn't make sense to dig into yesterday's treasure
when you only have the key for today,
for the things that make you smile and awake.
Every season asks of you a favor:
to shake hands and change for the better
in you and me.

Wounds hate when the rainbow takes you on a ride
and your eyes arise like the earth pushing out
a crystal from the place men don't dare to excavate.

It is harder to be a snake than to be a dove.
Everyone loves the purity of white,
but they forget that in the depth of black spaces,
I rescued my luminosity in my solitude.

Ain't no one perfect, dressed or naked.
But our human nature can hold hands forever.

I design myself to complement all of me.
Placing my being in all of you,
I have no other way, neither does the earth, to share with you.

The spirit of the earth is the mirror.
I look myself in the eye and pray.
Sketching out steps,
I paint the ladder into progress.

Healing starts when you pause
to create the next tune
that was missing your power song.

Shamanic Journey

Where I confess
and have internal dialogue,
where I find the rescue plan—

an inner flight
purchased with my intent,
the space that rescues me—

the quest for solutions,
the field where I rest,
where the petals of medicine shed—

where vision swims like goldfish
and hide like molly fish,
where I share what I consume.

Candles get lit,
and God gets dressed
as I undress.

Driven by ancient desire,
I keep alive the shamanic way.
I digest wisdom; what I can understand.

A space where my suffering is idolized
by helping my spirit to get ready
to raise my body—

where God leaves footprints
and birds empty their nests...
I recharge and take a break.

Where tornadoes
rip me apart and crow,
rebuild me—

where I learn from animals
that love me
like they depend on the source.

An inner flight
that sparks a question
that no longer lives in the mind.
I answer with sounds, symbols, and paintings
described by spirit.

A roll of a never-ending yoga mat,
a temple I can always visit,
the church I keep clean within me.

Invoking all good spirits
that fly with clean wings
and a sincere heart—

the piggy bank I always have to pull from
because I can't resist,
the feeling after my eyes released the string
that bonds me to spirit.

Burner of Borders
Cremator of Illusions
Burier of Wounds.

Lost child in the woods,
a gang of walking animals
with no leader.

Student of Wounds,
Master of Sealers,
Apprentice of The Great Mystic.

A post of my reflection,
Groomer of My Happiness,
Excavators of Simplicity.

Reclaiming my peace,
a tree sharing wisdom,
old rocks reflecting light.

A playground of mystery,
a slide of answers.
Landing in my new body,
I continue my journey.

In a personal dialogue with God,
a blessing from the elders,
playbooks made out of my dream.

Perseverance is my teacher,
and getting back up is a funny rope.
If you aren't tested by something,
there is no spiritual growth.

I pray for what you truly desire,
what fills up the vase
that I don't know how to sculpt.

A dance between myself and God,
a fly between the old me and the new me,
a game between oceans rising and water falling,
reliving emotional buildup.

A disciple seeking
what makes a warrior out of life,
the soul that never loses hope.

Shamanic journeying is
a flight between
what I didn't know,
and what I know now.

A hunting field of affirmations,
heaven of wisdom,
and field of visions.

Hypnotizing anxiety,
laying an axe on the bully bothering me,
reuniting myself with freedom.

A medium
that lets me see what am hiding from,
a canvas that unrolls me,
a brush that inspires a better me.

I am the easel I must fix.
The missing screw lies within.

If I keep God close to me
when my eyes are open

like when they are close,
then journeying
makes more sense to me.

So I call on the hands that
know what palette knife
must be rubbed on my ache.

So I call on the spirit
that flies in crows
and sleeps with rats
with no difference.

Have a meeting with the one
that doesn't live on time
and is always available to travel.

It's important to distinguish
when you are healed—
healing and no longer wounded.

Because everybody carries the medicine.
they need within,
so tap in and journey beneath
the flesh you came to this world in.

It's where I close my eyes
the light turned off
and my body vibrates, shaking off.

I can see the future me,
taking the present me on a dance

while the old me sings the song
that we move along to—

where I can see.
what I can't see
while my eyes are open,
a sensation...
I don't have to prove anything to anyone.

An outlet
to a world not really different from this one,
just a part of the same roots
that sprout different truths.

A research center,
an empty gallery...
Because I am the artwork
that has been worked on.

No one has names
or things to claim.
It's a field of oneness.

A meditation
that reveals and works
according to
what God believes I am ready for.

A messy backpack,
a chaotic art studio,
a pact train...
I'll never get bored
of visiting within.

Slow Down

God takes nine months to form life.
A caterpillar takes a day to meet the butterfly.
The seasons have their own calendar.

How do you understand the branch you are on
if you are dreaming of living on some other tree?

How do you understand the rocks you are on
if you are dreaming about the ocean?

How do you understand yourself
while living under some else's pace?

Death comes quick.
Make him wait
in line for your body.

Make the rush admire your patience.
Color blends quickly,
but it takes time to mold
into its final appearance.

Can you move at the speed
of your own body and not at the time
stress, bills, anxiety, and the rush clock you in at?

The Power of Smiling

Smiles massage the soul.
Flashlight your smile into my pupils.
to transmit songs of joy into my heart

A smile can uplift a tribe and give them hope.
Smiling, you make a turtle pop out,
hypnotize fishes,
make hermit crabs exchange souls instead of shells.

Let God sculpt you out of rockiness.
Making teeth happy
outside of a plaque soul.

Smile to build an empire
of spiritual guides blowing horns.

Fill a train with faces of smiling lips
and engage every single heart.

Knock out your heaviness,
sealing all exits
and permitting the entrance of joy and happiness.

Smile like a child next to a present
and a jar full of parental love.

Can I see the gum of your spirit
and the health of your energy?
Swipe all your being on Mother Earth;
She renews expired souls.

Become clay that wants to feel joy.
Spin your being into the bowl of life
and let the mystery of life build you out of the unknown.

Run all the miles you need while
you freestyle with the things that make you smile.
Become the textile God loves to wear.

Make chamomile smile before relaxation; keeps in.
Make smiling a worthwhile experience.
Bury all juvenile rage and hatred.
Grown-ups aren't always present.
Hungry crocodiles never pay attention.

Freestyle the song of love in your heart.
Find isles in everyone
with whom you can share your smile
because is not a sin
to share what makes you fertile?

Trust Yourself

Take your own hands for a walk.
Feel the earth naked barefoot;
The grass feels indifferent then.

The oil and water your skin produces...
Trust the changes you have no control over.
In those cycles, we can't afford to diverge.

Believe your letter arrived at the warehouse.
God processes and chooses
its most devoted devotees and seekers.

Be the garments awaiting their reveal.
Bask under the process.
Share the championship you acquire.
From the days you spend with trust meditating,
cry your soul out
and pamper yourself with the love
parents stare at their first child with.

Trust you aren't in control.
of who and what you love.
It doesn't matter when time is so short.
Piano your way into your own divinity.

Breathe in with the lungs of the mountain.
Each bird migrates to its creator.
Borrow wings and trust.
the reunion now.
Liberate what bones encage,

what muscles memorize,
and what aches the brain.

The heart is a button to rise and fall.
Press on it continuously.
Trust that God lives in the house you keep clean.
Velcro your veins to the one who lets no one down.
Stop being rushed by new releases and convenience.

Trust in the landscape of patience
and give your divine relationship
its definition.
Trust yourself once again.

When Do You Start Healing?

When you listen to your heart
and not the stomach that wants to eat all.

When you ask for divine help
and reach for the hand.

When you sail with the stream,
even when it takes you away from home.

When you reside in the mirror of compliments,
tattooing yourself with positive comments:
I am love and love is my home.
I am in love, not in fear.

When you become a still tree
and let your problems become bumper cars,
crashing into each other.

Let it be freely—
what's not letting you be free.

The First Hug of the Day

A reunion of bears making peace
with me in between,
a compressor
uplifting wrinkles—
a reminder that I come first.
Panda, teach me how to love myself.

Emotional blender,
magnetic touch...
a sensation that reminds me of baby clothes.
I know how I feel naked:
dressed and restful.

A touchdown,
a goal,
a home run
to know that I come first.

The gaze in the mirror...
I got your back, son.
Poetry is my shield
and a brush,
the autograph I share without a price.

The buckle lock,
the lock that has become rusty.
The best self-care is self-love.
The new squeeze out a hug.

I give myself the tightest hug.
To fill empty seats,
I shine light on me.

I satisfy my need first
before I sacrifice the rest of me.
I stare at everyone's eyes,

releasing internal tension.
I unlock the arms tied behind
souls bothered.

I nurture the mind with a good quote.
I hug myself like I did the first time I carried my son
and held his mother's hands.

Treat yourself like honeymoons.
Celebrate the spirit of Christmas daily
and wrap your body in the hug
 you give yourself.

Give yourself the first hug of the day.
Protect your energy.
Detoxify what naturally sticks to the skin.

Hug yourself like God holds the wand
that created all of this marvelous beauty.

Hug yourself
like musicians hold the mic,
a baby is held by mommy,
a snail sucks the soul out of glass.

Hug yourself
like new butterfly wings
touching the sky.

Hug yourself
like roots find their way in pots.

I know life is a fast-track,
but find ways to make her slow down.

Don't delay or betray
the hug that wants to become your friend.
Every day, spray yourself with love that's not far away.

A dry slice of bread
missing a touch of butter,
toasting love in the jam of today.

Can't you see that you are the first being
you must greet every morning?

Leave tracks and marks on
the stem on the tree of your body.

Juice the being beneath.
Place a light over the energy you need.
Love hates, greedy people. Be free!

Hug yourself like
kids hold on tight
before being released to kindergarten.

Breathe in the arms of God
into your chest.
Feel what it means to be healed.

Can't you see
how the breeze caresses the trees?

People judge me,
but I'm okay with that
because God compliments me,
and I'm cool with that.

So don't forget to kiss your body
with those hugs that you need first.

What the World Needs Now

A shamanic experience,
God as a coach,
a marriage with the earth.
Store no hate because that's just debt.
Embrace each other's colors.
See what nature has to say.
Balance solitude and express mode.
Think about you and me.
Turn off the bad news and meditate.
Converse about how God works instead of gossiping.
Send a DM to love.
Rise with the sun.
Read bedtime stories to the moon.
Be more human.
Embrace our life span.
Cherish a real talk.

We should walk in nakedness and be ourselves.
Prove no one but yourself wrong.
Hug, kiss, and talk.
March for affordable homes.
Knock the border down.

As we see the rainbow touch every landform,
discover love within
and treat the world with this luminosity.
Let God pop the bags under our eyes
so we get true rest,
where Life is a Spiritual Resort
and every day is a Super Bowl.
We can smile like my mother.

Fall in love with the now.
Steps out of the state
of whatever knocks us down.
Retrieve the last puzzle of nature
and remember God's footprints
on ancient land.

Wisdom is eager to be shared.
How do we get back up
with no special medicine
or prescription for that experience?

What the world needs now
is your compassionate input
and kind outlet.
Stop carrying all the weight
so we give someone a hand.
Take notes from the earth and the sky.
Exercise growth.
Be personal about your faith,
but be free with your practice.
Travel inwardly and rescue yourself
from emptiness and waste.

Be true to your glow
and master how to polish
so when you start to fade
you enjoy life as a playground.
Share your gift.
which is the self that just wants to be.

The world needs fewer wounds
and more healers;
less preachers,
more activists;
more prayers
and less distractions—
less drugs, more fruitful substance;
less careers and professions,
more liberated people;
more playtime and less slavery—
tickles and laughter,
rich beer and sweet wine,
relaxing teas and more decaf anxieties.

Let love rain on you and me.
Poetic reunions and flowers shaking off pollen.

Step away from race, culture, and surnames.
For a second, embrace oneness.
Gulp and savor the drink with no brand.
Claim nothing as ours.
Pause the repetition of nonsense.
Uplift the petal that craves truth,
need and desire,

The world needs a break
from tattoo imprints
and construction bruises.
Smell the flowers.
that make bees dance.
Think about the past.
Trust God as the hammock

that is an anchor to you.
Ask yourself:
When was last time we journeyed with God inside?
When was the last time I knocked on the door
and I heard a reply?
Why do we stop asking for help
after we see big checks
and things are fine?

The world needs more gardeners,
pruning, planting, sowing, and harvesting
a tomorrow
that we can all still ride a train in.
Give God reason to smile.

— Table of content —